STRESS MANAGEMENT

This new series is designed to meet the growing demand for current, accessible information about the increasingly popular wellness approach to personal health. The result of a collaborative effort by a highly professional writing, editorial, and publishing team, the *Wellness* series consists of 16 volumes, each on a single topic. Each volume in this attractively produced series combines original material with carefully selected readings, relevant statistical data, and illustrations. The series objectives are to increase awareness of the value of a wellness approach to personal health and to help the reader become a more informed consumer of health-related information. Employing a critical thinking approach, each volume includes a variety of assessment tools, discusses basic concepts, suggests key questions, and provides the reader with a list of resources for further exploration.

James K. Jackson	Wellness: AIDS, STD, & Other Communicable Diseases
Richard G. Schlaadt	Wellness: Alcohol Use & Abuse
Richard G. Schlaadt	Wellness: Drugs, Society, & Behavior
Robert E. Kime	Wellness: Environment & Health
Gary Klug & Janice Lettunich	Wellness: Exercise & Physical Fitness
James D. Porterfield & Richard St. Pierre	Wellness: Healthful Aging
Robert E. Kime	Wellness: The Informed Health Consumer
Paula F. Ciesielski	Wellness: Major Chronic Diseases
Robert E. Kime	Wellness: Mental Health
Judith S. Hurley	Wellness: Nutrition & Health
Robert E. Kime	Wellness: Pregnancy, Childbirth, & Parenting
David C. Lawson	Wellness: Safety & Accident Prevention
Randall R. Cottrell	Wellness: Stress Management
Richard G. Schlaadt	Wellness: Tobacco & Health
Randall R. Cottrell	Wellness: Weight Control
Judith S. Hurley & Richard G. Schlaadt	Wellness: The Wellness Life-Style

STRESS MANAGEMENT

Randall R. (Randall Russell) Cottrell

WELLNESS

A MODERN
LIFE-STYLE
LIBRARY

The Dushkin Publishing Group, Inc./Sluice Dock, Guilford, CT 06437

Russell
Russell

Library of Congress Catalog Card Number: 91-072188
Manufactured in the United States of America
First Edition, First Printing
ISBN: 0-87967-872-0

Library of Congress Cataloging-in-Publication Data

Cottrell, Randall R., Stress Management (Wellness)
    1. Stress (Physiology). 2. Stress (Psychology). I. Title. II. Series.
BF575.S75   616.89   91-072188   ISBN 0-87967-872-0

Please see page 145 for credits.

The procedures and explanations given in this publication are based on research and consultation with medical and nursing authorities. To the best of our knowledge, these procedures and explanations reflect currently accepted medical practice; nevertheless, they cannot be considered absolute and universal recommendations. For individual application, treatment suggestions must be considered in light of the individual's health, subject to a doctor's specific recommendations. The authors and the publisher disclaim responsibility for any adverse effects resulting directly or indirectly from the suggested procedures, from any undetected errors, or from the reader's misunderstanding of the text.

RANDALL R. COTTRELL

Randall Russell Cottrell was born in Oberlin, Ohio, in 1951. He is a graduate of Bowling Green State University, from which he received both a B.S. and an M.Ed., and the Pennsylvania State University, from which he received his doctorate in health education in 1982. He is currently Associate Professor and Head of the Department of Health and Nutrition Sciences at the University of Cincinnati. During the course of his professional career, Dr. Cottrell has written on a variety of health-related topics. In addition to his 2 titles in the *Wellness* series, Dr. Cottrell has published some 20 articles and is working on a text on worksite health promotion. As a speaker, he has addressed a diverse set of audiences including public school teachers, corporate executives, college students, mental patients, and Oregon forestry workers.

WELLNESS:
A Modern Life-Style Library

General Editors
Robert E. Kime, Ph.D.
Richard G. Schlaadt, Ed.D.

Authors
Paula F. Ciesielski, M.D.
Randall R. Cottrell, Ed.D.
Judith S. Hurley, M.S., R.D.
James K. Jackson, M.D.
Robert E. Kime, Ph.D.
Gary A. Klug, Ph.D.
David C. Lawson, Ph.D.
Janice Lettunich, M.S.
James D. Porterfield
Richard St. Pierre, Ph.D.
Richard G. Schlaadt, Ed.D.

Developmental Staff
Irving Rockwood, Program Manager
Paula Edelson, Series Editor
Maggie Hostetler, Developmental Editor
Wendy Connal, Administrative Assistant
Jason J. Marchi, Editorial Assistant

Editing Staff
John S. L. Holland, Managing Editor
Elizabeth Jewell, Copy Editor
Diane Barker, Editorial Assistant
Pamela Carley Petersen, Art Editor
Robert Reynolds, Illustrator

Production and Design Staff
Brenda S. Filley, Production Manager
Whit Vye, Cover Design and Logo
Jeremiah B. Lighter, Text Design
Libra Ann Cusack, Typesetting Supervisor
Charles Vitelli, Designer
Meredith Scheld, Graphics Assistant
Steve Shumaker, Graphics Assistant
Lara M. Johnson, Graphics Assistant
Juliana Arbo, Typesetter
Richard Tietjen, Editorial Systems Analyst

I ALWAYS BEGIN my stress management programs by asking members of the audience to stand up if they have ever felt their lives to be out of control or if they have ever felt the need for help in managing stress. To date, I have never had a member of any audience remain seated. Whether this is because today's life-style is more hectic and stressful than yesteryear's, or because people today are simply more aware of and concerned about stress, I do not know. What I do know is that virtually everyone I speak with seems to feel that he or she is overstressed and needs help in managing life.

As a result of this high interest in stress, there is a steady stream of books and articles on the topic. Not surprisingly, however, there is somewhat less than perfect agreement among the authors involved. Some claim that stress is nothing to worry about. Others single it out as the major cause of heart disease, cancer, and other serious maladies. One group claims that managing stress is as easy as remembering to tell a joke every day or to take a daily vitamin pill. Others argue that only individual counseling provided by a qualified therapist can help. The truth, I believe, lies somewhere between these extremes, and it is this point of view that informs this book.

This is not a definitive work, but rather a place to begin. It does not contain every available piece of information on stress, nor does it discuss every known stress management technique. Rather, it provides a basic introduction to stress, how it affects your health, and how it can be managed. The central objective of this books is not to make you into an instant expert but to help you learn to *think critically* about the conflicting information on stress which you will inevitably encounter. Only then will you be able to distinguish stress fact from stress myth, and only then will you be an informed health consumer.

Numerous people have had a role in the development of this book. I would like to thank Richard G. Schlaadt and Robert E. Kime of the University of Oregon for their roles in initiating the process that led to the publication of the *Wellness Series* and for their encouragement throughout. I would like to thank Irving Rockwood, Paula Edelson, Wendy Connal, and Jason J. Marchi of The Dushkin Publishing Group and Maggie Hostetler, the developmental editor, for their editorial assistance and continual guidance. A special thanks must go to Glen Schiraldi of the University of Maryland for his careful review of the manuscript and many useful suggestions. And most important, I must thank my wife, Karen, and my sons, Kyle and Kory. They are my support system, my inspiration, and my joy.

Randall R. Cottrell
Cincinnati, OH

Contents

1

Stress: An Introduction and Overview

Page 1

4

Controlling
Stressors

Page 69

5

Altering
Individual
Perception

Page 89

FIGURES

TABLES

Stress: An Introduction and Overview

S TRESS HAS BECOME an extremely prevalent issue in contemporary society. The modern world offers more opportunities and demands than ever before. One result is more people suffering from high levels of **stress**. But this phenomenon has led to a new awareness of the importance of techniques for coping with and managing stress. These techniques have improved countless lives by helping people place stress and the problems that cause it into proper perspective.

In strictly physiological terms, stress is a response caused by a direct stimulus, such as a snapping dog or a frightening pursuer. During such a response, the body experiences a series of physiological changes that put it into a state of high awareness. The brain and senses become alert, the heart beats faster, and our entire body mobilizes to help us ward off or run away from an attack. Because of this reaction, the **stress response** is often called the "fight-or-flight" response.

But although the body's stress response is designed to protect us from threats to our physical survival, it can have quite unhealthy effects. Many of the pressures people encounter in contemporary society are psychological: being late for an important meeting, being under pressure to meet a sales quota, or going through a divorce. These events are threatening but not physically menacing. They are, however, sufficient to trigger the stress response. If the resulting state of physiological arousal continues for any length of time, the body takes a beating. This kind of continual arousal contributes to a plague of stress-related illnesses, including **hypertension**, ulcers, migraine headaches,

Stress: Any disruption, change, or adjustment in a person's mental, emotional, or physical well-being caused by an external stimulus, either physical or psychological.

Stress response: The body's physiological response to stress that is triggered by the release of hormones; includes an increased heart rate and breathing rate, the diversion of blood to the muscles, and the release of fat from the body's stores.

Hypertension: The medical term for abnormally high blood pressure.

FIGURE 1.1
Fight or Flight Response: An Ancient Mechanism

Source: Collection of the Denver Art Museum.

The body's fight or flight response is designed to protect us from threats to our physical survival. This response is appropriate in the hunting scene in the cave painting above, but not to most pressures in contemporary society.

and heart disease. Learning to manage stress properly, therefore, is an important element of an effective disease-prevention strategy.

WHO EXPERIENCES STRESS?

Stress is not confined to the stereotypical harried executive, but affects everyone regardless of gender, age, race, or occupation. Even children are not immune. Fear of the dark, fear of the neighborhood bully, frustration at not being able to do what older children do, and sibling/peer rivalry are just a few examples of the many potential sources of childhood stress. To a child, such

FIGURE 1.2
Childhood Fears

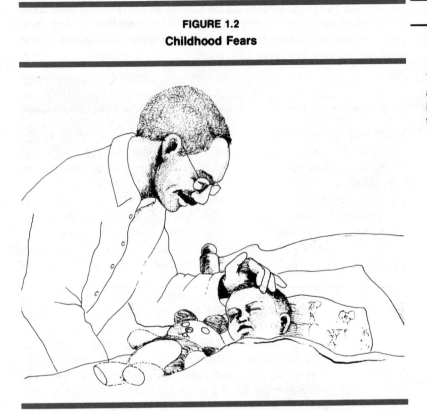

Childhood can be a stressful time of life. Adults can help by being sensitive to particular fears their children may have. If, for example, a child is afraid of the dark, it would be helpful to find ways of alleviating that fear by installing a night-light, reading a story before bed, or giving the child a favorite stuffed animal to sleep with.

Did You Know That . . .

Not all stress is bad. In fact, sexual arousal and the "fight-or-flight" stress response are physiologically similar, affecting the sympathetic nervous system in the same way.

problems are every bit as stressful as the problems faced by most adults. The many joys of childhood do not, alas, include freedom from stress.

Many people mistakenly believe that when they retire and leave the business world they will be free of debilitating stress. They are surprised to discover, however, that retirees also face plenty of stressful situations, such as financial problems, poor postretirement adjustment, failing health, and deaths of friends or loved ones. Retirees who have not developed outside interests with which to replace their jobs may be stressed by the resulting lack of stimulation. This stress, caused by lack of stimulation or activity, is called **deprivational stress** or underload. It can affect anyone, not just the elderly.

Deprivational stress: Stress caused by having too little stimulation or activity.

At the opposite end of the spectrum, some retirees become so involved in community service and volunteer activities that their pace seems just as hectic as it was before their retirement. These persons may suffer from **overload**.

HANS SELYE: THE FATHER OF STRESS

Overload: Stress caused by too much stimulation or activity.

Stressor: Any external demand or stimulus that triggers the stress response.

Distress: Stress caused by something negative or painful, such as a death in the family, being out of work, or failing a test.

Eustress: Stress caused by positive and enjoyable events, such as a job promotion, getting married, or competing in an important athletic event.

General Adaptation Syndrome (GAS): The general pattern by which the body adapts to stress over time. As described by Hans Selye (1907–1982), the GAS has three basic stages: the alarm reaction, resistance, and exhaustion.

Alarm reaction: The body's initial response to a stressor; the first stage of the General Adaptation Syndrome.

Resistance: Adjustments made by the body that allow it to maintain a high level of readiness in response to stress; the second stage of the General Adaptation Syndrome.

The Austrian physician Hans Selye is generally recognized as the "father" of stress. Selye was the first to borrow the technical term, stress, from the field of physics and apply it to a biological phenomenon. He defined biological stress as "the nonspecific response of the body to any demand made upon it." [1] He called it a "nonspecific response" because his studies found that any stress-arousing demand would elicit the same psychological response. The word "demand" in this context refers to a physical, psychological, or social stimulus. Another word for demand is **stressor**.

Stress is often considered a strictly negative phenomenon, but Selye thought otherwise. He believed that stress could be either positive or negative, and he developed terminology to distinguish the two. **Distress** is negative and painful. It may be caused by personal losses or setbacks, such as a death in the family, unemployment, failing a test, or simply because we are facing more demands than we can handle. **Eustress** is positive and enjoyable stress. It occurs when our stress levels are under control and we are experiencing maximum productivity, happiness, and health. Pleasurable activities and events, such as organizing a holiday celebration, getting a promotion, or competing in an important athletic event, may contribute to eustress. It is important to realize, however, that these same positive activities may become distressors if they are overdone or demand extra time from an already busy person.

Selye believed that the body responds to eustress and distress in the same way. This reaction, which Selye called the **General Adaptation Syndrome (GAS)**, involves 3 stages. [2] The first of these phases is the **alarm reaction**. Initially the body responds by using many of its reserves to create a state of hyper-readiness. If the stressor is too great, the body may become so depressed during the alarm reaction that it cannot recover, and death will occur.

Usually, however, the body rebounds from this state and enters the second stage, known as **resistance**. Now the body does everything it can to adapt to, and thereby resist, the stressor. The

**FIGURE 1.3
Hans Selye**

Did You Know That . . .

H ans Selye said, "Don't be afraid to enjoy the stress of a full life."

Source: Bettmann Archive.

Austrian-born physician Hans Selye (1907–1982) outlined the body's physiological reactions to stress in his General Adaptation Syndrome (GAS).

manifestations of this second phase are quite different from and, in some cases, the exact opposite of those occurring during the alarm reaction. For example, during the alarm reaction the cells of the adrenal glands secrete their contents into the bloodstream until they are depleted; during resistance, on the other hand, the cells of the adrenal glands become particularly rich in secretory material.

This increased resistance will continue until one of 2 things occurs: (1) the stressor is reduced or eliminated, allowing the body to return to normal; or (2) the body can no longer resist the stressor and proceeds into the third stage, **exhaustion**. This final

Exhaustion: The final stage of the General Adaptation Syndrome, characterized by the depletion of the body's stress-combating resources.

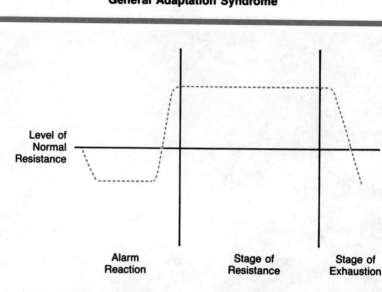

FIGURE 1.4
General Adaptation Syndrome

Selye noted that there is a pattern to the way in which people respond to stress. He described 3 distinct phases in his General Adaptation Syndrome: an alarm reaction, resistance to stress over time, and exhaustion.

phase finds the body's resources depleted. Fatigue sets in and the body becomes highly vulnerable to a variety of maladies. If the stress continues unabated, death may occur.

OTHER VIEWS OF STRESS

In recent years some experts have questioned Selye's pioneering work. In particular, many feel Selye may have overstated his theory of a "nonspecific" response. New studies indicate that different stressors may produce somewhat different responses. Although Selye used a variety of stressors in his laboratory experiments and they all produced the same response, the stressors he used did have one characteristic in common—they were all strange or unfamiliar. This common characteristic may account for the similar, and quite dramatic, responses that he observed.

The evidence of more recent studies has led psychologists and stress experts Myles and Sharon Genest to note that "the critical element in the development of stress is not any property of the stressor nor the physical response, but the individual's appraisal of the event and of her own ability to meet the demands presented by the event." [3]

As a result of these findings, stress can be defined better as an individual's response to a **perceived stressor**. Although individual perception may be the most important aspect of stress, it is important to understand all 3 phases of the stress response (alarm, resistance, and exhaustion) if one is to intervene and manage stress successfully.

STRESSORS

Some stressors are physical, such as extreme temperatures, dangerous activities, or bodily assaults. In today's society, however, physical stressors are the exception, not the rule. By far, the greatest number of modern stressors are psychological in nature.

Psychological stressors can be divided into 3 categories. The first of these, actual psychological stressors, refers to the stress caused by actually doing something perceived as stressful— for example, taking a test, preparing a budget, or making a presentation. Note that the term "actual" does not imply that the event or activity *should* be stressful. It simply is used to describe situations in which some real event or activity functions as a psychological stressor.

A second type of psychological stressor is the anticipation of an event. Worrying about a deadline that is approaching, dwelling on rumors that layoffs may occur at work, or thinking about a possible confrontation with a coworker are all examples of this type of stressor, which differs from actual psychological stressors because no event or activity is actually taking place. Instead, the individual is anticipating some future event that may or may not occur. Humans are the only species of animal known to experience stress caused by the anticipation of future events.

The third type of psychological stressor involves events that are totally imagined. In other words, there is no current event or activity that serves as the stressor, nor is any anticipated activity the cause of the stress. The entire stress reaction is created by the mind. Watching a frightening movie is an example of this type of stress. The members of the audience know they are perfectly safe.

Perceived stressor: A situation or circumstance (stimulus) that an individual recognizes as stressful.

Psychological stressors: Stimuli that cause psychological (as opposed to physical) stress.

Nevertheless, they can imagine themselves in the situation depicted on the screen and may experience a full-blown stress response.

Another imagined stressor occurs when people wake up in the middle of the night and think they have heard a noise in the house. Immediately, they start imagining all the worst-case scenarios, and the stress response kicks in.

In addition to physical and psychological causes of stress, emotions play a role in determining the stress response. Feelings of loss, anger, fear, anxiety, and loneliness can all create stress responses. These emotions may be responses to external events or may have developed within the individual. In either case, when stress responses occur, they are usually a combination of rational thinking and emotional responses.

Each individual has his or her own profile of stressors. The essence of stress management is learning to recognize those stressors and then finding effective means to deal with them. Later in this chapter we will look at some common causes of stress. It should not be considered an all-inclusive list, however, because there are many more stressors than we can mention here.

Personality Factors and Stress

In 1979 *Forbes* magazine identified 10 personality characteristics often exhibited by people with high stress levels:

1. A tendency to overplan each day so that if anything goes wrong or takes longer than anticipated, the day's schedule is thrown off;

2. A tendency to do several things at once, such as reading the paper, eating, watching television, and contemplating the evening's activities;

3. A stronger than usual need to win in both work and social activities so that even a harmless child's game, for example, can become a "do or die" situation;

4. A stronger than usual desire for advancement and recognition, sometimes leading to an unhealthy obsession with wealth and possessions;

5. An inability to relax without feeling guilty so that a work-related task must accompany any relaxation—for example, grading papers or reading briefs while watching television;

6. Impatience with delays or interruptions, including slower-paced coworkers or slow-moving cars;

7. A tendency to take on multiple projects with many deadlines, often leading to overcommitment at work and in social activities;

8. A chronic sense of time urgency—the feeling that there are never enough hours in the day to get done what needs to be done;

9. Excessive competitive drive—a tendency constantly to compare one's performance with that of friends, family, or co-workers;

10. Compulsion to overwork—the stress-prone person tends to ignore or underemphasize all aspects of life that do not involve work. Stress-prone individuals are usually the first to arrive at the office and the last to leave. When they finally do leave, they take their work home with them. These are the people often referred to as **workaholics**.

The cardiologists Meyer Friedman and Ray Rosenman were among the first to notice the behaviors characteristic of a stress-prone personality. They labeled those people **Type A**. Those who were more easygoing and who could easily relax were considered **Type B**.

People with Type A personalities are more prone to heart diseases and **strokes** than those who are Type B. In fact, Friedman and Rosenman have observed that nondiabetic, nonhypertensive people with normal cholesterol and Type B personalities are nearly immune to **coronary heart disease**. [4]

Life Events

It has been said that the one sure thing about life is change. Unfortunately, studies have shown that life changes can contribute to stress and stress-related illnesses. Psychiatrists Thomas Holmes and Richard Rahe developed a scale to measure life changes. When they tested their scale, they were able to show that the greater the degree of life change, the greater the chance of illness. Those people scoring 150 to 199 on the scale showed a 37 percent chance of illness the following year, those scoring 200 to 299 showed a 51 percent chance, and those scoring over 300 showed a 79 percent chance.

Daily Hassles

Taking the life-event theory one step further, the psychologist Richard S. Lazarus has hypothesized that everyday **hassles** may

Workaholic: Someone who compulsively devotes as much time as possible to his or her work and lacks interest in or is unable to find satisfaction in other activities.

Type A: A behavior pattern or personality type; the typical Type A individual is hard-driving, highly competitive, hostile, verbally aggressive, easily angered, extremely time-conscious, and unable to relax.

Type B: A pattern of behavior typical of individuals who are relatively relaxed or easy-going; often defined in contrast to Type A.

Stroke: Damage to part of the brain caused by interruption in its blood supply; stroke may result in physical or mental impairment or even death.

Coronary heart disease: A reduction in blood supply to the heart caused by narrowing or blockage of the coronary arteries; often results in temporary or permanent damage to the heart muscle.

Hassles: Relatively minor but frequently encountered stressors, such as rush-hour traffic or long lines at the bank or store, that are sources of annoyance on an everyday basis.

FIGURE 1.5

Type A vs. Type B Personalities

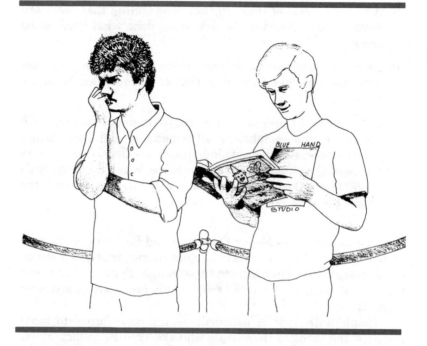

Frustrations in life, such as having to wait in line, are more easily handled by those who are laid-back and relax easily (B-type personalities) than those who are impatient and stress-prone (A-type personalities).

be even more detrimental to health than major life events. Hassles are those chronic nagging stressors that occur on a regular basis. Examples include automobile problems, troublesome neighbors, disruptive children, difficulty paying the bills, and an impossible boss.

Lazarus also hypothesized that daily **uplifts**—positive events that make us feel good—would serve to protect us from stress and counterbalance the daily hassles. Although the absence of uplifts has not been found to be related to poor health, the presence of hassles has. Hassles have been found to be predictive of psychological distress and to be related to poorer states of both physical and mental health. Furthermore, preliminary evidence seems to support Lazarus's hypothesis that daily hassles are more detrimental to health than major life events.

Uplifts: Positive events that create pleasure, serve as protection from stress, and counterbalance daily hassles.

(continued on p. 16)

Wired for Stress

[On Oct. 19, 1987,] a day that only a stress researcher could savor, a 48-year-old stock-broker named Gianni Fidanza happened to be wearing a little metal box on his waist when he went to his Park Avenue office. It was wired to a cuff on his arm that measured his blood pressure and pulse every 15 minutes. The device came from the cardiovascular center at New York Hospital-Cornell Medical Center, where scientists, led by cardiologist Thomas G. Pickering, are using this new technology to record stress directly in the workplace. Black Monday gave them a wonderfully tidy result: the Dow Jones industrial average correlated inversely with Fidanza's blood pressure and pulse.

After the first hour of trading, the Dow was down 93 points and Fidanza was up 86 (if you added up the increases in his pulse and blood pressure). As Fidanza, one of the two principal brokers at the Euram Securities Corporation, watched prices tumble on the Quotron screen and tried to calm his clients on the phone, his pulse rose to 83 beats per minute from 64. His blood pressure, which had been 132 over 87 earlier that morning, hit 181/105. His subordinates started watching the machine on his waist, Fidanza recalls. "They decided it was as good as the Quotron for following the market."

At first glance, there was nothing surprising about this. Here was the classic model of stress, a male executive reacting to a challenge in the corporate jungle, pumping adrenaline, flooding his arteries, maybe slowly killing himself in the process. For more than 25 years, studies of male executives have been showing that the price of corporate success can be a heart attack. Recently, though, researchers have started looking at the nonexecutive victim of stress, and it's these other studies that make the Black Monday results look surprising.

For it turns out that decision-making male executives may actually have it relatively easy. It's the underlings—secretaries, assembly-line workers, waitresses and other order-takers—who are emerging as the burn-out cases, especially women who have to worry about children after work. If you think it was stressful being a brokerage executive during the biggest one-day drop in the history of Wall Street, try spending a perfectly ordinary Wednesday with an administrative aide/support staff supervisor named Cathy Collins.

A nonscientist could argue that you didn't need the monitor that earlier had been strapped to Cathy Collins's waist to know she was feeling stressed at 10:26 A.M. on the Wednesday in question. There were other clues, such as the fact that she had just finished muttering, "I've got to get away from here before I slit my wrists." By this time she had been awake for five hours. She had set out bagels and cereal for her two children; left her home in Teaneck, N.J., and arrived two bus rides later at her desk in a tiny, windowless cubicle at New York Hospital's cardiology unit. Since then, there hadn't been a quiet moment.

The phones rang, of course; some files had been misplaced, an unscheduled patient arrived, a secretary had called in sick, to the irritation of others (Collins promised to have a word with the missing secretary about her pattern of absenteeism). Collins kept answering calls for her boss, Jeffrey Borer, a cardiologist in charge of two cardiac laboratories.

At 10:26 A.M., she was standing, the phone cradled on her shoulder, and contending with the following:

- One patient at her desk, waiting to talk to her.
- One secretary with a question about another patient's chart.
- Two lighted buttons on her telephone, indicating incoming calls, and one buzzing intercom.
- Two forms on her desk, which she was filling out as she punched back and forth between phone calls.
- A three-inch-thick stack of paperwork in her "In" box, above which she had taped a sign, "Lack of planning on your part does not constitute an emergency on my part."

• Her boss, who had just emerged from his office with a sheet of paper and said, "Cathy, I need this Xeroxed right away, please."

At that moment, a beep sounded, the machine at her waist started drawing in air, and the cuff on her arm tightened. The monitor showed her pulse, which had been 71, to be 82; her blood pressure was 116/72. (Researchers don't agree which of these three numbers is the best indicator of stress, but the one that has traditionally received the most attention is the diastolic blood pressure—the second figure given, in this case, 72—which is used to diagnose hypertension. It measures pressure in the arteries between heart beats; the other reading, the systolic pressure, here 116, measures peak pressure while the heart is pumping.) Collins's diastolic pressure had risen 26 percent, an even greater percentage change than Fidanza had registered that first hour of Black Monday. And, as it turned out, this wasn't even the biggest surge of the day for Cathy Collins.

Were these surges dangerous? Would Collins one day be coming to her own office as a cardiac patient? Now, at age 34, she didn't seem at risk—unlike many blacks, who tend toward high blood pressure, she has quite low results, and even her peak diastolic pressure in the office was well below the danger range (which starts at about 90). But many researchers suspect that continual stresses may eventually contribute to permanent high blood pressure as well as to other afflictions—strokes, atherosclerosis, heart attacks—that seem to be the byproducts of modern Western civilization.

What Collins underwent at 10:26 is called a "fight-or-flight" reaction: a surge of blood pressure, adrenaline and energy to prime the muscles for action. Researchers theorize that the walls of the arteries can thicken when the muscles are stretched by frequent rises in blood pressure; thicker walls mean less room for the blood and higher pressure. The arteries can also become clogged with deposits of cholesterol plaque, which seem to accumulate more readily on arterial walls that have been damaged by sudden pressure increases and by repeated doses of corrosive stress hormones. Stress also adds cholesterol to the bloodstream—for instance, cholesterol levels in tax accountants rise dramatically just before April 15.

Studies of monkeys have demonstrated the long-term effects of stress on the arteries. The anthropologist Jay R. Kaplan and the psychologist Stephen B. Manuck at the Bowman Gray School of Medicine in North Carolina looked at different groups. In some, the dominant male held his position for two years—no newcomers were introduced to challenge him. In others, new monkeys were added periodically, forcing the dominant male to fend off challengers, and it was these continual strugglers who ended up with the most severely clogged arteries. In a follow-up study, some dominant monkeys were given beta-blocker drugs that damped the rising of their blood pressure and pulse; this time, their arteries didn't clog (even though they remained as aggressive as ever).

In humans, though, the link between the fight-or-flight reaction and heart disease hasn't been so easy to demonstrate. Researchers have looked at "hot reactors"—people who show marked increases in heart rate, blood pressure and stress-related brain chemicals and hormones, such as adrenaline and cortisol, when exposed to stress (such as playing a video game or dunking a hand in ice-cold water) in the laboratory. Some studies show that hot reactors are more prone to heart disease; but the evidence is mixed, and some scientists doubt that dunking someone's hand in cold water in the laboratory will tell you very much about what happens in daily life.

And so, recently, many researchers have gone into the field, measuring blood pressure and adrenaline in places ranging from villages in Samoa to Volvo assembly lines in Sweden. The portable monitor on Cathy Collins's waist is one of the most promising new tools, a chance to finally get a simple numerical measurement of what happens in the real world.

Every 15 minutes, when the beeper sounded, Cathy Collins noted in a diary what she was doing and checked off how she felt: happy, sad, angry, anxious. Studies at Cornell have shown that women's blood pressure peaks when they're anxious (whereas for men it's when they're angry), and Collins fit the trend. Her peak reading at the office—a diastolic pressure of 77—came in the morning when she was mediating a dispute between two secretaries over who had made a mistake with a report. She hit this level again just before lunch when she was in that perennial secretarial bind: politely taking orders from someone who annoys you.

In this case, it was a patient, a tense, well-dressed suburban matron convinced that something was wrong with her despite repeated tests showing she was healthy. She prevailed on Collins to make the calls setting up appointments with specialists. At that moment, there were two real emergencies going on—doctors were rushing in and out of the office to consult about a woman near death on an operating table, and a cardiac patient from another hospital needed to be transferred by helicopter to the medical center. In the midst of all this, Collins spent 15 minutes negotiating appointments for the matron; her voice remaining pleasant, but her diastolic pressure peaking and her pulse hitting 90.

"I was pretty annoyed," she said afterward. "I know I should be tolerant of hypochondriacs—if there's a mental problem it can make you feel physically ill—but I don't like being forced to spend so much of my time on cases like that when I've got so many other things to do that seem more constructive."

What she was facing at this moment, according to a new paradigm in stress research, was the worst kind of situation: a "high-strain" task. The paradigm was developed by Robert Karasek, an industrial engineer at the University of Southern California. He defines stress on the job according to the demands of the task (how fast-paced and chaotic the workplace is) and the amount of control a worker has. This produces four categories of jobs.

The low-demand, low-control category would be someone like a night watchman. Then there are workers in calm, orderly environments who have lots of control in deciding when and how they do something; the ideal example is a forester (assuming there's no forest fire going on),

and others might be architects, natural scientists or car mechanics.

The harried executive falls into a third category: high demand, high control, which would also include doctors, newspaper reporters and some teachers. As a principal stockbroker at his firm, Fidanza may have felt his world was going out of control on Black Monday, but he could still decide how to direct his subordinates, how to spend his own time, what advice to give clients. And this control seems to be good for the heart, according to Karasek. "When you have freedom to decide how to act, you can perceive the job's demands as positive," he says. "They're challenges, opportunities to learn new strategies." Karasek's studies show that executives don't suffer more heart disease than average.

It's the workers in Karasek's fourth category who really seem to be suffering. These are switchboard operators, assembly-line workers, waiters, receptionists, typists, short-order cooks, garment stitchers—anyone who faces constant demands but has little control in deciding how to meet them. Karasek calls these high-strain jobs and thinks the resulting frustration produces the surges in blood pressure that Cathy Collins underwent when all the phone lines were blinking, when something had to be photocopied that instant, when she had to put aside her work to make phone calls for the suburban matron. And Karasek thinks that many workers have it worse than Collins, because she at least has many other moments in the day when she can decide how and when to do things.

"The really stressful jobs," Karasek says, "are some of these new pink-collar specialities like the data-entry person in the word-processing pool, or the clerk who only does endless, meaningless filing, or the office Xerox operator. We've taken the job of the traditional secretary, who has some latitude in deciding what skills and strategies to use, and broken it down into jobs where the person has to do the same thing over and over. When you couple that low control with a high demand—for instance, when typists know they have to do a certain number of keystrokes per hour—your'e liable to see stress-related illnesses."

Evidence of this illness comes from nine

studies that include some impressively large samples of subjects—5,000 men across America, 958,000 men and women in Sweden. Except for one contrary result in Hawaii (where job strain didn't seem to affect disease rates), the studies show that rates of heart disease are higher than average among workers in high-strain jobs—as much as four times higher than those of low-strain workers even allowing for the fact that high-strain people smoke more than average. (Researchers suspect their smoking habits are partially a result of frustration at work.)

New evidence comes from the portable monitors at Cornell, which were worn by 210 New York men at all levels of responsibility to their jobs at the city's Department of Sanitation, Bloomingdale's, The Daily News, New York Hospital, Joseph E. Seagram & Sons, Drexel Burnham Lambert and the Federal Department of Health and Human Services. The Cornell researchers, cardiologist Pickering and cardiovascular epidemiologist Peter Schnall, find that men in high-strain jobs, such as clerical positions and machine operations, are five times more likely than the others to have hypertension (defined as an average diastolic pressure on the job above 90).

"The $64,000 question," Pickering said, "is what this chronic stress on the job does over the long term. Your body recovers quickly from short-term stress—in a few minutes the blood pressure comes back down. But if this goes on continually, we suspect that eventually your system may change, and your blood pressure will remain elevated." Pickering and Schnall are planning to test this thesis by tracking the 210 New York men for the next five years to see whether the high-strain workers' blood pressure rises more than that of the others.

Another Cornell researcher, the anthropologist Gary James, has started studying working women—who, not so incidentally, hold a disproportionate number of high strain jobs.

Cathy Collins was one of 120 technical and clerical workers at New York Hospital asked to wear the monitor for a 24-hour period, and her readings certainly seemed to confirm the job-strain hypothesis.

It was a typical Wednesday for her, yet her blood pressure rose throughout the day as much as Fidanza's did on Black Monday. (It could be argued, of course, that having a reporter around all day—and a photographer on another day—would be enough to raise anyone's blood pressure. For this reason, Collins's readings on those days are not being used in James's study. But these readings were no higher—in fact, they were slightly lower—than on the day she'd worn the monitor for the study.) Collins's average diastolic pressure at the office, not counting the 20-minute break she took to eat a crab salad lunch, was 64. This was 23 percent higher than her resting blood pressure (as measured during her sleep), roughly the same percentage rise as Fidanza's on Black Monday.

There was one crucial difference, though, between the stockbroker and the administrative aide. After Fidanza walked home on Black Monday, he relaxed. He sat down to watch television with his wife, and his blood pressure dropped 20 points from what it had been when he left the office. He had no pressing responsibilities that night—his children are grown and living elsewhere—and his blood pressure tapered off during the evening. But when Cathy Collins left the office at 5 o'clock to take a bus home to her split-level house in Teaneck, there were new stresses awaiting her arteries.

By dinnertime, Cathy Collins's blood pressure was higher than it had been all day at the office. She had picked up her 10-year-old daughter, Candra, at ballet school, gotten home, and suddenly realized that Candra had missed a piano lesson. After an apologetic phone call to reschedule the lesson, she was about to call another parent to arrange a car pool for the weekend, but then her husband, Andrew, an advisory resource planner in middle management at I.B.M., arrived and she got distracted by the questions of what he should pack for his trip to Atlanta in the morning, and what should go in the washing machine now, and what the children would have for lunch tomorrow. Then her son, André, age 16, came into the kitchen to ask for help with his test the next day on "Romeo and Juliet," and there were potatoes to peel and a pot roast to heat, and then—anyway, by the time the family sat down to eat, her diastolic blood pressure was up to 80.

It dropped during dinner, but then there were new strains. She was planning to take her daughter to a meeting of Jack and Jill, an academic and social organization for middle- and upper-middle-class black families, on Saturday, but her husband insisted that Candra was grounded this weekend for using his comb and brush.

"All right," said Cathy Collins, "she's grounded except for that meeting. I've already paid $30 for it."

"No, she's not going," said her husband. "She broke one of the rules I made. If I came home and found André using my cologne, I'd ground him, too."

"Well," said Candra, "if you're talking about your cologne, André *has* been using it." This produced an angry denial from André, another argument, and soon Candra was sobbing in her mother's arms. The question of the meeting Saturday was put aside—there were dishes to clean up and a bed to be changed upstairs. At 9:34, Collins's blood pressure was back up to 79, again higher than it had ever been at the office.

As she changed the bed, Cathy Collins told a reporter that Candra's outburst at the table had made her feel guilty. "I think one reason the kids get upset is that I work. I'm not always here when the children want me around, and it bothers me, so I make a special effort to schlep them around and find things for them to do on the weekend. I don't want them to get bored. It's not their fault I have to work to make a living."

Researchers would call this a textbook case of dual-role conflict, a problem that's attracted attention as more women have started working outside the home. Women were generally ignored in the early days of stress research—after all, it was men who were suffering most of the heart attacks and working in the high-power jobs. But although women are less prone to heart attacks (perhaps because of such hormones as estrogen and progesterone), heart disease still kills 250,000 women a year. Women suffer almost as many strokes as men, and are more prone to depression, which is probably linked to stress. Researchers suspected these problems would increase as more women entered the workforce, but recent studies have shown this isn't necessarily true. Women who work outside the home, in fact, tend to be slightly healthier on the average than those who do not.

But some women seem to be at especially high risk—the ones who combine a high-strain job with housework and family responsibilities. Suzanne Haynes, an epidemiologist with the National Institutes of Health, studied 737 women in Framingham, Mass., and found that the women with especially high rates of heart disease were married clerical workers, and the risk went up with each additional child in the home. Another N.I.H. epidemiologist, Andrea LaCroix, found that high-strain jobs caused more heart problems for the women in Framingham than for the men. And Gary James's study of technical and clerical workers at New York Hospital shows that the women's diastolic blood pressure correlates with the number of children at home—the more children, the higher the pressure.

"We talk about husbands and wives sharing the burden at home, but it still seems to be women who have the most to cope with," says James. "They get home from work and they can't relax. They have all these responsibilities to meet in a few hours, and you see their blood pressure doesn't follow the typical pattern of tapering off in the evening. It's what you see with Cathy Collins. As stressful as her job is—and I've seen what a madhouse her office can be—for her the big challenge of the day seems to be in the evening."

James bases this not just on Collins's blood pressure readings on the particular Wednesday he observed—when Collins's pressure averaged 70 in the evening, or 10 percent higher than at the office—but also on the stress-related chemicals coursing through her bloodstream. From urine samples, James determined that she was producing twice as much adrenaline at home than at the office.

Should Cathy Collins be worried about what's surging through her arteries? At the moment, probably not. For one thing, she already has enough to worry about. For another, she may have some biological protection against heart disease, since her blood pressure is well below average. And, perhaps most important, she seems to enjoy what she's doing.

At 9:35, after changing the bed and before going to help her children with homework, she sat down for a moment and smiled, thinking back on her long day. "I like being busy at the office. I feel more productive, the time passes quickly, and when work's over I'm pretty good at leaving it behind me." It was easy to believe her—throughout all the day's crises, she had never really looked overwhelmed, and there was even some supporting data from the monitor.

Perhaps the final judgment on the day came after she went to bed at 11:30, the monitor still hooked up to the cuff on her arm. The nighttime readings give a clue to one of the key questions: How much does stress really get to someone? Researchers can measure what kinds of environment are stressful, and they can suggest general ways to ease the strain, such as giving workers more control of their jobs. But ultimately, of course, stress is in the mind of the stressed. "I guess the best advice I can offer," James says, "is, 'Don't let the turkeys get you down.' It's normal for your blood pressure to shoot up when there's a challenge—that's healthy. You may need the extra energy at that point. What's worrisome is when the stress keeps eating at you afterwards, and your blood pressure just won't go down."

By midnight, the ringing phones and demanding patients and family arguments were apparently gone; Collins's blood pressure was down to 43, just over half of what it been earlier in the evening, and she was sleeping soundly. The only stress that really affected her that night, she said later, was the cuff that kept inflating around her arm.

Source: John Tierney, *New York Times Magazine* (5 May 1988), pp. 49, 81–85.

Job-Related Stress

Unsurprisingly, some of the most intense stressors stem from factors related to one's job. Situations that may cause this type of stress include impossible deadlines, competition among colleagues, unclear job responsibilities, supervising (or not supervising) others, and difficult interpersonal relationships. The effects of these job-related stressors vary from person to person, often depending on individual personality characteristics and personality type.

Symptoms of job stress include job dissatisfaction, low **self-actualization**, and low **self-esteem**. As with other forms of stress, the consequences of stress on the job depend in large part on the individual's response. If, for example, that response involves an increase in smoking, then the consequences could include all the health risks that go with heavy use of tobacco including an increased risk of cardiovascular disease, lung cancer, hypertension, and higher levels of **blood cholesterol**. It would be unfair and inaccurate to say in such a case that all of the above effects were directly caused by job stress. Nonetheless, job-related stress can and does serve to trigger behaviors that in turn have negative health effects for many people.

Self-actualization: A state in which one has realized his or her fullest potential by developing all of his or her capabilities to the greatest extent possible; associated with the personality theorist and psychotherapist Abraham Maslow (1908–1970).

Self-esteem: The value an individual places on him- or herself; one's feeling of self-worth.

Blood cholesterol: The level of cholesterol—a fatlike substance found in animal foods and also manufactured by the body—found in the blood.

(continued on p. 18)

You've got an important project to finish, but your thoughts keep drifting away because you and your spouse had an argument last night or your daughter is struggling with her schoolwork.

Or it could be that you were ready to leave for your son's stage debut when the facsimile machine delivered a rush purchase order that you had to act on.

Stress! Stress! More Stress!

Then, there's the two-places-at-once syndrome. How often have you taken the red-eye flight because you didn't want to miss an important family activity the night before a business trip?

Welcome to stress in the '90s. "Stress may be the biggest management headache of the 1990s because it's so difficult to detect," says attorney Paul Siegel at the New York office of Jackson, Lewis, Schnitzler & Krupman.

Yet, unquestionably, stress is costly to business. More than 1 million days of absenteeism and more than $20 billion in workers compensation costs each year can be traced to stress, says Mr. Siegel. And that doesn't include overtime needed to cover workers who are absent because of stress or accidents that occur because people are worried and get careless.

How can a company reduce workplace stress? Its human-resources managers must make management aware of the ten most frequent causes of stress in the workplace, said Mr. Siegel at a Jackson, Lewis seminar in Boston last month.

First, there are what Mr. Siegel calls the "high-tech helpers—the damned fax overnight mail, and the new computer."

"You now get an endless stream of fax mail that forces you to act immediately. There is no time to delegate it or research it." Then, there are computer breakdowns or the installation of a new computer system coupled with minimal training of your employees. "The machine just looks at you," says Mr. Siegel. "It can't talk."

Second, there is the difficulty of supervising people with drug and/or alcohol problems. "You try to be helpful and supportive, but often rehabilitation is really enabling behavior that lets an individual continue his habit," says Mr. Siegel. "You get to the point where you want to kill the person. Then guilt sets in, and you're stressed out."

A third cause: supervisory malfunction. "No one trains supervisors, and then they malfunction because they are used to *doing,* and don't know how to communicate or supervise," says Mr. Siegel.

A fourth stress factor: quotas and deadlines in combination with reduced staff levels. "Companies are trying to do more with less," he says. "And then when there is absenteeism, all of a sudden there aren't enough workers."

Work environments—too hot, too cold, or equipment that's too old

Today's fast-paced decision-making can create near-constant stress. Experts theorize that, 25 years ago, managers had time to relax and regroup between business crises.

or too new—can cause stress as well as corporate policies that deal with issues like smoking, drugs, or AIDS. "AIDS is scary for the person who has it, and the person who doesn't have it," says Mr. Siegel.

Diminishing workplace privacy is another common cause of stress. "Today's technology makes it easier for companies to monitor keystrokes, telephone calls, and letters received and sent," says Mr. Siegel. "Does the company have the right? Yes. Does it have a need? Probably. Does it make people more comfortable? No."

In addition, the merger-acquisition craze has left people more insecure about their jobs. In the past, says Mr. Siegel, employees could count on a good relationship with a supervisor for job security. But in the aftermath of a takeover the new boss is often someone with a brand-new M.B.A. who doesn't know what anyone can do.

The last two workplace causes of stress: Fear of not keeping up, and the two-places-at-once syndrome, where people worry about meeting both family and work obligations.

Companies also need to discover workplace-specific causes of stress. "Find out in exit interviews why people quit," says Mr. Siegel. "Often it's stress from poor supervision, or drugs in the workplace."

If a company is going to reduce stress in the workplace, it needs to both be aware of the causes of stress and have a program to help stressed-out workers.

Mr. Siegel suggests setting up an employee-assistance program and running grievances through the personnel department. "An open-door policy that says come see the boss when you have a problem will never work."

Also, employees should get feedback, and supervisors should get employee-rights training. "Employees want a voice. Otherwise, they will churn on their job frustration," says Mr. Siegel. "And supervisors must be taught not to do things such as yell at someone in front of another co-worker or personalize criticism with comments such as 'You idiot!' "

Source: Michael A. Verespej, *Industry Week* (5 June 1989), p. 19.

Experts estimate that stress-related problems and mental illness cost businesses $150 billion annually in health insurance and disability claims, lost productivity, and other related expenses. More than 90 percent of the 500 largest companies already have in place some form of employee assistance or wellness program designed to help employees manage stress. [5]

To manage stress-related problems effectively at the work site, however, companies must go beyond simply supplying stress management programs for employees. They need to examine the changes that could be made in the work environment itself to reduce stress. Employee child care, more flexible work schedules, and participatory management, for example, may contribute just as much to reducing stress as teaching stress-management skills to individual employees.

Stress at Home

By providing a social support system, a solid family life with close interpersonal relationships and good communication can be the cornerstone of stress management. On the other hand, strained family relationships can be highly stressful and can cause emotional trauma and fatigue that may be severely debilitating. [6]

Stress levels may be quite high in a single-parent home where one person must take on all the roles and responsibilities usually handled by two. The same may be true in a home in which traditional sex roles are strongly maintained and the man takes little responsibility for parenting and home maintenance and upkeep. Probably the least stressful homes are those in which all family members—including children—share domestic responsibilities.

Another factor that can lead to stress at home is the physical environment. Is the neighborhood dangerous? Is it overcrowded? Is it too noisy? Any of these situations can cause domestic stress, destroying the peace and relaxation one expects to enjoy in one's home.

Where you live is another potential stressor. Most ratings have assumed that the places with the best climates and the best economic and cultural conditions are the best places to live. Psychologist Robert Levine disagreed with that assumption. His rankings of cities in the United States are based on a factor he labeled the "city stress index." (See next page.)

College-Life Stressors

The college years can be one of the most enjoyable times of life, as students experience new freedoms and independence as well as new responsibilities. It can also be a time of extreme stress caused by a heavy academic work load, fear of academic failure, and stiff competition for good grades and admission to graduate schools. In addition, many students must pay part or all of their college costs, which requires a careful balancing of job and school responsibilities. Poor nutrition and substandard living conditions also may increase stress for those students struggling to make it through college financially.

Another source of college stress is the pressure many feel to make life decisions relating to career, marriage, or even child-

(continued on p. 26)

Did You Know That . . .

Though parents may think going to the dentist or gaining a new sibling are children's greatest stressors, psychologists believe that hearing their parents fight creates the worst stress in kids.

City Stress Index

Rating the best place to live is an old American tradition. According to the *Places Rated Almanac,* back in the 17th century, promoters of Maryland tried to persuade colonists to choose their state over Virginia with statistics showing that you could enjoy meatier turkeys, shoot more deer and suffer fewer deaths from disease and Indian massacres simply by settling on the northern shores of Chesapeake Bay. Today's raters work with considerably more data and more sophisticated statistical methods, but their results provoke even more debate.

As *Time* magazine pointed out in 1985: "Whether the subject is the beefiest burger or the biggest corporation, Americans have a penchant for making lists of the best and worst, then arguing about the results. . . . No rankings have inspired more disagreement than those about home sweet home."

When my own hometown came up dead last a few years ago—Fresno was rated "the worst city in America" by geographer Robert Pierce in 1984—I decided to follow the lead of the legendary psychologist E. L. Thorndike, who once devised his own "goodness of life" measure of American cities. He advised, "Do not take anybody's opinion about your city. Get the facts."

The rankings that recently generated the greatest flap came from Richard Boyer and David Savageau's *Places Rated Almanac* and from Pierce's reworking of their data. Boyer and Savageau took statistics that described climate and terrain, housing, health care, crime, transportation, education, the arts, recreational facilities and economic conditions in each metropolitan area and then averaged the nine scores to come up with an overall "quality of life" score for each area.

Pierce, a geographer at the State University of New York at Cortland, criticized the way Boyer and Savageau's ratings lumped together the scores from all categories as if they were equally important. He had 1,100 New Yorkers rank the nine criteria on the basis of how important each

was in deciding where to live and used these rankings to weight the factors into a revised quality of life index.

According to Boyer and Savageau's 1985 ratings, the 10 best places in the country to live were Pittsburgh, Pennsylvania; Boston, Massachusetts; Raleigh-Durham, North Carolina; San Francisco, California; Philadelphia, Pennsylvania; Nassau-Suffolk, New York; St. Louis, Missouri; Louisville, Kentucky; Norwalk, Connecticut; and Seattle, Washington. The 10 worst were Yuba City, California; Pine Bluff, Arkansas; Modesto, California; Dothan, Alabama; Albany, Georgia; Benton Harbor, Michigan; Gadsden, Alabama; Casper, Wyoming; Rockford, Illinois; and Anderson, Illinois.

In Pierce's 1985 ratings, the 10 best areas were Nassau-Suffolk, New York; Raleigh-Durham, North Carolina; Norwalk, Connecticut; Knoxville, Tennessee; Asheville, North Carolina; Pittsburgh, Pennsylvania; Johnson City-Kingsport-Bristol, Tennessee; Charlottesville, Virginia; Louisville, Kentucky; and Boston, Massachusetts. The worst were Pine Bluff, Arkansas; Flint, Michigan; Rockford, Illinois; Yuba City, California; Peoria, Illinois; Benton Harbor, Michigan; Baton Rouge, Louisiana; Janesville-Beloit, Wisconsin; Casper, Wyoming; and Racine, Wisconsin.

"Les chiffres sont les signes de Dieu" ("Statistics are signs from God"), according to Prior Roger Schultz of Taize. Perhaps. But do these particular signs really assess the quality of life in different cities? The rankings assume that people who live under better environmental, economic and cultural conditions are more satisfied with their lives. But psychologists have long recognized that favorable living conditions don't always produce subjective well-being. And the places-rating studies have virtually ignored any direct measure of well-being.

Researchers Kuni Miyake, Marta Lee and I felt that any comprehensive assessment of the best and worst places to live should certainly include this in its calculations. We designed our own study, comparing the same metropolitan areas of the United States on the best measures we could find of well-being.

There are no good statistics reflecting the "psychological health" of metropolitan areas, but there are reliable data for four important indicators of psycho-social pathology: rates of alcoholism, suicide, divorce and crime. We chose these measures because they are both causes and effects of social stress, clearly an important element in psychological well-being.

Both the best and the worst cities in our ratings (see charts) had a single dominating institution, but of very different kinds. State College, Pennsylvania, which had the least pathology, is socially, economically and architecturally built around Pennsylvania State University. Juris Draguns, a psychology professor there, points out that the city's work force has been dictated primarily by the needs of the university, producing what he describes as "a highly educated, predominantly middle- and upper-middle-class population. . . . There are no acute community controversies, no major unresolved problems and no explosive uncontrolled growth."

At the other extreme, Reno and Las Vegas, Nevada, were first and second in overall pathology, based on alcoholism, suicide and divorce rates that were considerably higher than the rest of the country. Even without the divorce figures, which are inflated by the presence of so many people who come to Nevada just to get a divorce, the two cities would still be highest in overall pathology. This is no surprise, given the gambling centers' freewheeling frontier reputation. The social norms of such casino-dominated cultures—which encourage risk-taking and escape from reality, while handing out free drinks—undoubtedly foster pathology in both visitors and residents.

When we compared our rankings statistically to those in the other studies, there was virtually no correlation. Even looking just at the top and bottom 10, for example, neither of the other rankings had any of the same cities we did on our list. And of the six cities that appeared on both the other top-10 lists—Pittsburgh, Boston, Raleigh-Durham, Louisville, Norwalk and Nas-

sau-Suffolk—only Nassau-Suffolk appeared anywhere in our top 25.

To see how our findings applied to larger areas of the country, we combined the metropolitan area figures on pathology and came up with some surprising results. The West and the South, known for their mild climates and easy living, ranked highest and second highest respectively on all four types of pathology. The cities of the north central region were ranked third in everything except for alcoholism, on which they ranked last, followed by the Northeast.

The sharp differences between our rankings and the others indicate that the objective environmental, economic and cultural conditions they use as guidelines don't relate very well to pathology. When we compared their rankings with the alcoholism, suicide, divorce and crime rates in each city, the correlations were very weak.

We then thought that perhaps some of their nine objective measures might tie in with pathology, if we could just find the right ones. So we took the five that seemed most relevant—population, population density, climate, average income and overall economic vitality—and calculated the relationship of these measures, both separately and in statistically derived combinations, to pathology.

These results were even more surprising. Pathology often seemed to go along with better conditions rather than worse. Higher suicide and crime rates, for example, were associated with milder climates and healthier economic conditions. These findings recalled a warning offered years ago by the late Angus Campbell. After dedicating much of his career to studying psychological well-being, Campbell concluded that "we cannot understand the psychological quality of a person's life simply from a knowledge of the circumstances in which that person lives."

Why is this? Why do better conditions so often go with worse mental health? Perhaps, we thought, Boyer, Savageau and Pierce had matters the wrong way around. Perhaps good conditions do not prevent pathology but attract it. We know that moving to a new area often appeals to

Getting Riled About Ratings

When Robert Pierce ranked American cities at the 1984 meeting of the Association of American Geographers, his findings provoked a record-breaking number of phone calls. The hullabaloo surprised Pierce. "It's rather astonishing," he said, "the degree of interest this type of research generates." Later, after CBS produced *Fresno* as a prime-time spoof of *Dallas,* Pierce noted that his study "was probably the first in the history of academic geography to produce a television spinoff."

Responses to Richard Boyer and David Savageau's rankings have been no less intense. "We get a lot of mail about our book," they quipped, "some of it ticking."

One reason for the fuss is that ratings can translate to profits or losses. When Greensboro tied for first with Knoxville in Pierce's 1984 ranking, the president of the Chamber of Commerce admitted, "We capitalized on it. We mentioned it in ads placed in different magazines and periodicals around the country."

The losers, on the other hand, have paid a stiff price. "These unsolicited surveys that are done by somebody because they want to do a survey and release it publicly can be absolutely devastating to a city's economy," observed former Tulsa, Oklahoma, Mayor Terry Young. When clerical errors from one such study resulted in an undeserved low ranking for Tulsa, the city filed a $26 million lawsuit (dropped after the error was corrected) against the researcher for defaming the city's reputation.

Other reactions to the 1985 rankings, compiled in *Rating Places,* were equally strong and equally predictable:

"I've lost about two weeks of my life returning telephone calls to irate citizens. I think it should be illegal for this type of analysis to be completed."
  —Mayor Bill Hurley of Fayetteville, N.C. (ranked 145th)

"It's not that we don't deserve to be No. 1. It's just that we're simply not used to being on top in anything that doesn't involve football. Now we have every reason to fear a Yuppie invasion. As you know, Yuppies take lists and ratings very seriously."
  —Peter Leo, columnist, The Pittsburgh Post-Gazette

"Yes, it is a good place if you are earning $25,000 a year, love winter and adore potholes."
  —Letter to *Time* magazine from a Pittsburgh resident

"Pittsburgh is kind of like Newark without the cultural advantages."
  —Johnny Carson

"Yuba City [ranked last] isn't evil. It isn't bad. It's just not very much."
  —Richard Boyer, ratings-maker

"We're planning a little get-together on the 10th Street bridge to burn Rand-McNally [publisher of *Places Rated Almanac*] maps."
  —Ron Haedicke, county fair manager, Yuba City

people who are having trouble in their lives and think that a fresh start somewhere may help them. So they move to a place where conditions are most attractive, bringing their pathology with them and driving up the rates of divorce, suicide, alcoholism and crime in these areas.

We also know that moving itself can create problems, even for people who were doing well before they moved. Sociologists have found that areas with large concentrations of migrants suffer from what they call "social disorganization." New arrivals often have trouble meeting new situations and new social norms, find themselves in conflict with their new neighbors and must deal with the loss of relationships that had supported them in the past. Instead of finding peace, they face new stresses and strains, which often lead to further problems.

(box text continues on p. 26)

The 25 Lowest Stress Cities

Overall Rank	Metropolitan Area	Lowest in Alcoholism	Least Crime	Fewest Suicides	Least Divorce
1	State College, PA	1	33	8	20
2	Grand Forks, ND	38	9	1	52
3	St. Cloud, MN	44	3	16	15
4	Rochester, MN	6	17	19	66
5	McAllen/Pharr/Edinburg, TX	48	102	6	11
6	Altoona, PA	73	7	77	3
7	Bloomington, IN	4	61	3	182
8	Provo/Orem, UT	8	24	40	30
9	Utica, NY	29	8	26	34
10	Akron, OH	11	114	53	7
11	Sheboygen, WI	10	20	61	37
12	Lancaster, PA	10	10	73	36
13	Paterson/Clifton/Passaic, NJ	32	105	48	2
14	Bismarck, ND	5	12	179	32
15	Allentown/Bethlehem/Easton, PA	69	29	134	4
16	Lafayette/West Lafayette, IN	25	22	5	169
17	Nassau/Suffolk, NY	34	38	47	23
18	Poughkeepsie, NY	40	53	30	38
19	Albany/Schenectady/Troy, NY	58	19	170	5
20	Lawrence, KS	2	167	14	161
21	New Bedford/Fall River, MA	55	163	4	26
22	Bloomington/Normal, IL	17	64	20	108
23	Wheeling, WV	85	1	51	76
24	Cumberland, MD	65	2	69	72
25	Wausau, WI	58	19	94	29

If your city isn't in the top 25, you'll find it somewhere on the next two pages. Seek and ye shall find.

26) Pittsfield, MA: 112, 56, 12, 42—27)Iowa City, IA: 4, 100, 87, 87——28) Bryan/College Station, TX: 16, 166, 9, 71—29) Johnstown, PA: 19, 31, 197, 16—30) York, PA: 32, 18, 126, 53—31) Eau Claire, WI: 38, 16, 114, 74—32) Steubenville, OH/Weirton, WV: 104, 14, 33, 93—33) Williamsport, PA: 12, 21, 162, 91—34) Fargo, ND/Moorhead, MN: 46, 28, 123, 51—35) Sioux Falls, SD: 18, 36, 100, 110—36) Binghamton, NY: 39, 13, 165, 73—37) Janesville/Beloit, WI: 26, 106, 50, 64—38) Grand Rapids, MI: 48, 138, 17, 83—39) Waterloo/Cedar Falls, IA: 21, 68, 76, 102—40) Brownsville/Harlingen/San Benito, TX: 52, 148, 25, 46—41) Green Bay, WI: 7, 43, 229, 47—42) Laredo, TX: 109, 179, 103, 1—43) Fort Collins, CO: 30, 78, 36, 132—44) Florence, AL: 126, 30, 7, 184—45) Reading, PA: 19, 31, 233, 31—46) Dubuque, IA: 119, 41, 113, 18—47) Syracuse, NY: 168, 67, 45, 57—48) Lincoln, NE: 15, 88, 99, 86—49) New London, CT/Norwich, RI: 49, 53, 58, 140—50) Abilene, TX: 143, 129, 101, 10—51) Erie, PA: 97, 55, 81, 60—52) Sharon, PA: 62, 6, 222, 41—53) Harrisburg, PA: 14, 50, 196, 67—54) Parkersburg, WV/Marietta, OH: 55, 25, 110, 137—55) Cedar Rapids, IA: 62, 71, 160, 24—56) Saginaw, MI: 112, 185, 65, 14—57) Lima, OH: 65, 104, 55, 80—58) Danville, VA: 263, 5, 18, 48—59) Buffalo, NY: 129, 93, 67, 54—60) Fort Smith, AR-OK: 27, 62, 10, 272—61) Lorain/Elyria, OH: 71, 45, 89, 128—62) Canton, OH: 71, 58, 95, 106—63) Kenosha, WI: 127, 126, 29, 50—64) Fort Wayne, IN: 50, 70, 105, 113—65) Madison, WI: 109, 84, 63, 68—66) Sioux City, IA-NE: 96, 77, 49, 117—67) Manchester/Nashua, NH: 91, 53, 74, 144—68) Joplin, MO: 58, 49, 52, 213—69) Champaign-Urbana/Rantoul, IL: 23, 170, 60, 121—70) Decatur, IL: 58, 123, 22, 196—71) Anaheim/Santa Ana/Garden Grove, CA: 148, 153, 156, 8—72) Lansing/East Lansing, MI: 20, 122, 108, 136—73) Pascagoula/Moss Point, MS: 209, 44, 21, 238—74) Pittsburgh, PA: 143, 66, 142, 25—75) New Haven/Waterbury/Meriden, CT: 117, 120, 46, 84—76) Elmira, NY: 76, 42, 174, 107—77) Kokomo, IN: 42, 173, 13, 281—78) Boston, MA: 115, 230, 41, 19—79) Newport News/Hampton/Norfolk/Va. Beach, VA: 219, 158, 11, 35—80) Springfield/Chicopee/

Holyoke, MA-CT: 98, 228, 56, 21—81) Youngstown/ Warren, OH: 116, 133, 75, 55—82) Burlington, VT: 129, 27, 167, 95—83) Fayetteville/Springdale, AR: 35, 35, 78, 209—84) Alexandria, LA: 212, 73, 212, 6—85) Trenton, NJ: 94, 222, 57, 45—86) Newark, NJ: 85, 257, 31, 22—87) Bremerton, WA: 58, 60, 171, 157—88) Glens Falls, NY: 67, 40, 258, 40—89) Omaha, NE-IA: 80, 166, 64, 124—90) Jersey City, NJ: 141, 254, 15, 27—91) Minneapolis/St. Paul, MN: 94, 118, 149, 79—92) Mansfield, OH: 73, 186, 23, 214—93) Rochester, NY: 155, 122, 104, 58—94) Bridgeport/Stamford/Norwich/Danbury, CT: 150, 135, 96, 56—95) Columbia, MO: 13, 183, 166, 139—96) Jacksonville, NC: 137, 144, 85, 70—97) Florence, SC: 213, 244, 2, 86—98) Hagerstown, MD: 115, 48, 224, 59—99) Albany, GA: 229, 147, 151, 9—100) Tuscaloosa, AL: 178, 165, 28, 97—101) Portsmouth/Dover/Rochester, NH-ME: 123, 23, 194, 146—102) Elkhart/Goshen, IN: 77, 32, 154, 240—103) Bangor, ME: 132, 60, 155, 123—104) Athens, GA: 109, 131, 136, 75—105) Clarksville/Hopkinsville, TN-KY: 102, 76, 54, 244—106) St. Joseph, MO: 36, 146, 119, 202—107) Kankakee, IL: 246, 150, 83, 89—108) Kalamazoo, MI: 28, 201, 62, 230—109) Davenport/ Rock Island/Moline, IA-IL: 44, 101, 204, 145—110) Philadelphia, PA-NJ: 178, 181, 102, 33—111) Johnson City/Kingsport/Bristol, TN-VA: 162, 15, 214, 135—112) Greeley, CO: 132, 274, 141, 63—113) Vineland/Millville/Bridgeton, NJ: 123, 205, 138, 39—114) Victoria, TX: 135, 193, 27, 194—115) Chicago, IL: 208, 168, 59, 62—116) Killeen/Temple, TX: 53, 75, 86, 271—117) Amarillo, TX: 150, 187, 252, 12—118) Gary/Hammond/ East Chicago, IN: 152, 157, 80, 119—119) Providence/ Warwick/Pawtucket, RI-MA: 214, 125, 130, 49—120) Hartford/New Britain/Bristol, CT: 129, 233, 42, 105—121) Evansville, IN-KY: 75, 107, 98, 257—122) Bellingham, WA: 170, 98, 106, 155—123) Oxnard/Simi Valley/Ventura, CA: 189, 89, 97, 158—124) San Angelo, TX: 42, 173, 161, 224—125) Hickory, NC: 238, 83, 117, 90—126) Columbus, OH: 68, 193, 140, 198—127) Montgomery, AL: 186, 94, 38, 243—128) Peoria, IL: 75, 128, 200, 171—129) Medford, OR: 140, 74, 111, 246—130) Burlington, NC: 272, 69, 37, 142—131) Springfield, MO: 52, 118, 180, 237—132) Ann Arbor, MI: 25, 184, 221, 188—133) Battle Creek, MI: 194, 172, 35, 172—134) Owensboro, KY: 184, 40, 153, 223—135) Knoxville, TN: 135, 47, 169, 242—136) Midland, TX: 119, 216, 82, 167—137) Duluth, MN/Superior, WI: 173, 26, 271, 77—138) Milwaukee, WI: 202, 99, 198, 65—139) Jackson, MS: 197, 191, 150, 185—140) Charlottesville, VA: 233, 81, 176, 78—141) Lake Charles, LA: 159, 195, 181, 61—142) Salem, OR: 62, 165, 207, 179—143) Muncie, IN: 82, 86, 122, 273—144) Flint, MI: 222, 63, 147, 165—145) Springfield, IL: 129, 231,

79, 170—146) South Bend, MN-IN: 80, 175, 157, 228—147) La Crosse, WI: 156, 65, 279, 28—148) Lewiston/ Auburn, ME: 120, 82, 242, 152—149) Des Moines, IA: 99, 177, 208, 141—150) Wichita Falls, TX: 123, 220, 24, 268—151) Monroe, LA: 143, 140, 232, 101—152) Dayton/Springfield, OH: 248, 208, 93, 201—153) Chico, CA: 227, 137, 84, 156—154) Longview/Marshall, TX: 175, 150, 135, 189—155) Atlantic City, NJ: 139, 282, 68, 17—156) Shreveport, LA: 197, 226, 121, 88—157) Terre Haute, IN: 87, 51, 280, 153—158) Cincinnati, OH-KY-IN: 184, 152, 195, 98—159) Eugene/Springfield, OR: 78, 110, 226, 234—160) Melbourne/Titusville, FL: 125, 176, 178, 190—161) Chattanooga, TN-GA: 204, 136, 90, 212—162) Washington, DC-MD-VA: 170, 238, 120, 92—163) Ft. Walton Beach, FL: 85, 34, 209, 277—164) Topeka, KS: 152, 160, 236, 103—165) Austin, TX: 89, 178, 201, 220—166) Sherman/Denison, TX: 91, 174, 133, 267—167) Jackson, MI: 146, 169, 215, 143—168) San Antonio, TX: 138, 226, 125, 200—169) Charleston, WV: 240, 72, 172, 173—170) Baton Rouge, LA: 100, 272, 148, 96—171) Toledo, OH: 194, 159, 190, 122—172) Texarkana, TX-AR: 82, 96, 227, 264—173) Tyler, TX: 105, 139, 270, 109—174) Colorado Springs, CO: 102, 190, 255, 118—175) Honolulu, HI: 65, 116, 164, 129—176) Nashville, TN/Davidson, NC: 163, 154, 185, 206—177) Racine, WI: 184, 180, 216, 100—178) Benton Harbor, MI: 192, 224, 131, 149—179) Charleston/North Charleston, NC: 236, 265, 44, 81—180) Yakima, WA: 209, 197, 109, 103—181) Anniston, AL: 189, 203, 43, 263—182) Spokane, WA: 165, 108, 223, 211—183) Boise City, ID: 135, 113, 168, 270—184) Vallejo/Fairfield/Napa, CA: 206, 142, 188, 187—185) Fayetteville, NC: 264, 207, 70, 126—186) Macon, GA: 274, 86, 88, 216—187) Muskegon/Norton Shores/Muskegon Heights, MI: 106, 270, 173, 120—188) Tallahassee, FL: 211, 212, 137, 162—189) Asheville, NC: 282, 38, 203, 133—190) Rockford, IL: 197, 211, 143, 186—191) Lynchburg, VA: 247, 57, 266, 85—192) Portland, ME: 204, 97, 248, 164—193) Great Falls, MT: 200, 90, 177, 258—194) Louisville, KY-IN: 223, 132, 152, 219—195) Raleigh-Durham, NC: 277, 112, 139, 138—196) Hamilton/Middletown, OH: 165, 118, 230, 229—197) Enid, OK: 202, 103, 186, 248—198) Anderson, SC: 161, 152, 261, 131—199) Kansas City, MO-KS: 115, 248, 192, 192—200) Wilmington, DE-NJ-MD: 237, 199, 206, 82—201) Salt Lake City/Ogden, UT: 181, 20, 243, 166—202) Anderson, IN: 121, 112, 99, 282—203) El Paso, TX: 189, 240, 144, 181—204) Pine Bluff, AR: 32, 217, 128, 283—205) St. Louis, MO-IL: 244, 236, 115, 116—206) Beaumont/Port Arthur, TX: 168, 239, 92, 255—207) San Jose, CA: 178, 183, 210, 210—208) Gadsden, AL: 242, 79, 182, 251—209) Birmingham, AL: 221, 202,

116, 232—**210**) Indianapolis, IN: 167, 161, 118, 275—**211**) Waco, TX: 173, 216, 189, 217—**212**) Greenville/Spartanburg, SC: 235, 223, 159, 160—**213**) Salinas/Seaside/Monterey, CA: 251, 198, 127, 191—**214**) Baltimore, MD: 192, 280, 124, 69—**215**) Augusta, GA: 257, 109, 163, 218—**216**) Las Cruces, NM: 200, 256, 72, 215—**217**) Modesto, CA: 214, 209, 187, 177—**218**) Olympia, WA: 23, 80, 284, 250—**219**) Seattle/Everett, WA: 204, 218, 184, 203—**220**) Billings, MT: 132, 92, 273, 233—**221**) Greensboro/Winston-Salem/High Point, NC: 273, 144, 199, 111—**222**) Visalia/Tulare/Porterville, CA: 244, 204, 202, 125—**223**) Cleveland, OH: 216, 206, 247, 104—**224**) Biloxi/Gulfport, MS: 269, 92, 205, 197—**225**) Santa Barbara/Santa Maria/Lompoc, CA: 210, 171, 244, 178—**226**) Santa Cruz, CA: 175, 142, 260, 199—**227**) Bradenton, FL: 154, 195, 265, 163—**228**) San Diego, CA: 197, 196, 251, 151—**229**) Richmond/Petersburg, VA: 226, 188, 249, 115—**230**) Pensacola, FL: 159, 259, 107, 256—**231**) Columbus, GA-AL: 245, 95, 193, 260—**232**) Fresno, CA: 279, 262, 39, 150—**233**) Lubbock, TX: 89, 274, 225, 204—**234**) Wilmington, NC: 276, 253, 71, 147—**235**)

Corpus Christi, TX: 225, 245, 129, 221—**236**) Gainesville, FL: 159, 277, 112, 227—**237**) Casper, WY: 178, 155, 132, 279—**238**) Lawton, OK: 242, 211, 34, 276—**239**) Savannah, GA: 231, 275, 32, 235—**240**) Detroit, MI: 231, 273, 175, 94—**241**) Fort Myers, FL: 262, 112, 238, 209—**242**) Columbia, SC: 225, 268, 183, 130—**243**) Huntsville, AL: 83, 130, 282, 266—**244**) Charlotte/Gastonia, NC/Rock Hill, SC: 271, 233, 158, 180—**245**) Portland, OR: 151, 266, 228, 207—**246**) Wichita, KS: 159, 214, 256, 253—**247**) Memphis, TN-AR-MS: 251, 263, 145, 175—**248**) Denver/Boulder, CO: 182, 243, 263, 159—**249**) Galveston/Texas City, TX: 265, 229, 272, 43—**250**) Daytona Beach, FL: 258, 247, 220, 127—**251**) Sarasota, FL: 197, 134, 281, 226—**252**) Pueblo, Co: 278, 222, 245, 114—**253**) Mobile, AL: 219, 267, 146, 245—**254**) Roanoke, VA: 255, 87, 283, 134—**255**) Dallas/Fort Worth, TX: 171, 258, 211, 249—**256**) Yuba City, CA: 229, 220, 254, 225—**257**) Tulsa, OK: 235, 190, 231, 265—**258**) Redding, CA: 281, 118, 213, 254—**259**) Atlanta, GA: 252, 237, 241, 195—**260**) Albuquerque, NM: 284, 262, 276, 13—**261**) Santa Rosa, CA: 253, 127, 275, 222—

The 25 Highest Stress Cities

Overall Rank	Metropolitan Area	Lowest in Alcoholism	Least Crime	Fewest Suicides	Least Divorce
262	Tucson, AZ	210	252	253	231
263	Tacoma, WA	240	213	259	236
264	Stockton, CA	283	251	191	176
265	Riverside/San Bernardino, CA	270	260	234	148
266	Houston, TX	233	255	219	247
267	New York, NY	249	286	66	44
268	Tampa/St. Petersburg/Clearwater, FL	216	264	246	239
269	Bakersfield, CA	268	271	218	193
270	Ocala, FL	266	241	240	241
271	Sacramento, CA	219	249	277	208
272	Orlando, FL	187	278	237	259
273	Oklahoma City, OK	260	235	239	261
274	Phoenix, AZ	257	232	267	252
275	Fort Lauderdale/Hollywood, FL	247	269	278	183
276	West Palm Beach/Boca Raton, FL	255	281	257	154
277	Los Angeles/Long Beach, CA	275	284	235	112
278	San Francisco/Oakland, CA	267	276	268	174
279	Jacksonville, FL	262	227	262	274
280	Odessa, TX	178	279	217	280
281	Panama City, FL	260	246	250	284
282	North Little Rock/Little Rock, AR	167	242	264	284
283	Lakeland/Winter Haven, FL	280	250	269	262
284	Miami, FL	248	285	274	205
285	Las Vegas, NV	285	283	285	285
286	Reno, NV	286	201	286	286

So it may be that the very attractiveness of conditions in the West and South—mild climates and a slower pace of life—lures people prone to pathology, who in turn create a social milieu that fosters more pathology. To test this idea, we examined the relationship between pathology rates and 1980 census data that showed the percentage of people in each city who had moved from some other state. We found that the higher migration rates of the Sunbelt areas of the South and West went with correspondingly higher rates of alcoholism, suicide, divorce and crime, whether we compared cities or regions.

Clearly there is no simple connection between objective living conditions and the psychological quality of your life. "The mind is its own place," wrote John Milton in *Paradise Lost*, "and in itself can make a heaven of hell, a hell of heaven."

Robert Levine, "City Stress Index: 10 Best and 10 Worst," *Psychology Today* (November 1988), pp. 53–58.

bearing. Interpersonal stressors are also common between boyfriends and girlfriends, roommates, professors and students, and employers and employees. Add to all this the typical student's level of involvement with societal concerns, clubs and organizations, intramural sports or interscholastic activities, and the like, and it is easy to understand the potential for stress-related problems and the need for good stress management skills among college students.

Biological Causes of Stress

Along with the many psychosocial causes of stress, several biological factors can influence the stress response. Caffeine and nicotine both cause a physiological reaction very similar to that caused by stress. Sugar consumption and some vitamin deficiencies may affect stress reactions adversely. Noise, whether unexpected, disruptive, or continuous, can also stimulate the physiological mechanisms of the stress response. Disruption of body rhythms, such as that caused by moving across several time zones in a short period of time (jet lag), can be very stressful. **Premenstrual syndrome** has also been shown to have a significant impact on the way some women react to stress.

Hardiness

Some researchers have turned their attention to the study of personality traits that may protect people from stress. In trying to discover why occupational stress causes illness for some workers but not for others, the psychologist Suzanne Kobasa found 3 personality factors that seem to be common among those who are best able to cope with occupational stress. These are control, challenge, and commitment. When found together, they constitute what Kobasa describes as **hardiness**.

Premenstrual syndrome: A combination of emotional and physical symptoms, including irritability, tension, and fatigue, that occurs in some women prior to the onset of menstruation; popularly known as PMS.

Hardiness: A term used to describe a set of personality characteristics found in certain people who tend to cope well with stress. Hardiness comprises 3 distinct qualities sometimes referred to as the 3 C's: commitment, challenge, and control.

Hardy individuals perceive themselves to be in control of their situation. They do not feel helpless but instead believe they can prevent, terminate, or reduce the severity of negative events. Hardy individuals also see obstacles as positive challenges rather than negative roadblocks. They believe that change and struggle are normal and that they can obtain personal growth and a sense of accomplishment by overcoming life's difficulties.

In addition, hardy individuals are committed to their jobs or whatever task is at hand. They believe in what they do, and they try to involve themselves in life rather than allowing themselves to become alienated, threatened, or passive. In related research, psychologist Raymond Flannery studied night school students who were in situations that seemed highly stressful. Many were working full-time jobs, raising families, commuting long distances through city traffic, and taking classes. Surprisingly, many in this group seemed perfectly happy and showed no signs of being stressed. Based on an examination of frequency of illness and reported symptoms of **anxiety** and **depression**, he divided the group into those who were "stress-resistant" and those who were not. He then studied a number of psychological and behavioral variables for the 2 groups.

Essentially, he found 4 main differences between the stress-resistant group and those who reported a greater incidence of illness, anxiety, and depression. First, like Kobasa's hardy individuals, those who were stress-resistant maintained personal control in their lives and were also committed to a goal of some kind. The stress-resistant persons also made relatively little use of substances such as alcohol, nicotine, or caffeine; they engaged in regular aerobic exercise, and they took at least 15 minutes every day to relax and do some activity they enjoyed. Finally, the stress-resistant group tended to seek out other people, whereas the illness-prone group tended to be more socially isolated.

In essence, both hardy and stress-resistant persons held a common perception of life that maximized the positive and minimized the negative. Not only does this finding provide further evidence of the importance of perception in stress, but it also can help us identify individuals who may be prone to stress-related illness. Flannery believes that the coping skills typical of his stress-resistant people can be taught, and he is developing programs to teach such skills.

Since Hans Selye first borrowed the term "stress" from the field of physics to describe an observation in his laboratory, the field of stress management has grown rapidly. Experts now view stress as a highly complex phenomenon involving a stressor,

(continued on p. 30)

Did You Know That . . .

Some psychologists believe people can be taught to be hardy. Trainees learn such coping strategies as perceiving situations more positively, locating specific causes of feelings, and learning to live with stressors that can't be changed.

Anxiety: An emotional state characterized by general uneasiness, apprehension, or fear.

Depression: A mental state characterized by extreme sadness or dejection that persists for an extended period of time.

Evaluating Your Own Stress Level

Deciding whether you need to do something about stress is easier if you have an accurate assessment of your own stress level. A good way to begin is simply by asking yourself whether you feel stressed. The answer may be obvious.

If it's not, or if you'd like independent confirmation of your intuitive judgment—perhaps coupled with a more detailed analysis—it's time for the next step. Precisely what that step should be will depend on your situation. One possibility is to obtain and use one of the currently available assessment tools that are designed to help you identify trouble spots. One of these is Stress-Map®, a stress analysis questionnaire. The complete StressMap® questionnaire contains 21 scales similar to the 3 excerpted here. The excerpt below

reproduces 3 of these 21 scales—namely those pertaining to personal changes, pressures, and satisfactions.

To use this excerpt from StressMap®, first circle the number that best describes your response to each statement. Once you have answered all the questions in a given scale, add your scores vertically. Then, add those totals horizontally and write the resulting "scale total" in the large circle at the lower right of the scale. Once you have done this, find and darken the small circle in the column of circles above your scale total whose numerical range includes your score. Finally, turn to page 30 and follow the instructions there to complete the exercise and compile your own sample StressMap®.

SCALE 4   PERSONAL CHANGES

Think about . . . the past **year.** For each of the changes listed below, indicate how much each has been a source of stress to you.

	Great	Moderate	Little	None/ Didn't Occur		
Change in residence	3	2	1	0		
Death of a close family member or friend	3	2	1	0		
Crisis with friend/family member (drug problem, job loss)	3	2	1	0		
Separation or divorce of family member	3	2	1	0		
A new close relationship	3	2	1	0		
Your separation or divorce	3	2	1	0		
Home improvement or repair	3	2	1	0		
Illness or injury keeping you at home for a week or more	3	2	1	0		◯
Change in family activities	3	2	1	0	4	
New family member (birth, adoption)	3	2	1	0		◯
Serious illness in family	3	2	1	0		
Financial loss or diminished income	3	2	1	0	10	
Major personal achievement	3	2	1	0		◯
A major purchase or new debt	3	2	1	0		
A "falling out" in a family or friendship	3	2	1	0	18	
Involvement in legal system	3	2	1	0		◯
Property loss, theft, damage, or accident	3	2	1	0		
Crime victim	3	2	1	0		

——— + ——— + ——— + ——— = ◯

Scale 4 Total

NOTE: The term *family* is used generically to mean those people close to you, your inner circle, and not necessarily a traditional family. The word *mate* is used generically to mean spouse, significant other, or life partner.

SCALE 5   PERSONAL PRESSURES

Think of . . . the past **year.** For each of the pressures listed below, indicate how much each has been a source of stress to you.

	Great	Moderate	Little	None/Didn't Occur
Not enough money	3	2	1	0
Heavy debts	3	2	1	0
Conflicts with mate	3	2	1	0
Conflicts over household tasks	3	2	1	0
Problems with children/housemate	3	2	1	0
Pressures from in-laws, family	3	2	1	0
Not enough time with family/friends	3	2	1	0
Work-family conflict	3	2	1	0
Sexual conflict or frustration	3	2	1	0
Dangerous or stressful neighborhood	3	2	1	0
Few friends in neighborhood	3	2	1	0
Time pressures with mate	3	2	1	0

4 ○

9 ○

15 ○

○

_____ + _____ + _____ + _____ = ○

Scale 5 Total

SCALE 6   PERSONAL SATISFACTIONS

Think about . . . the people closest to you and your experience with them in the past **month.** To what degree is each of the following statements true of these relationships?

	Very	Somewhat	Little	Not At All
The people around me will take time for me when I need it	3	2	1	0
Those closest to me understand when I am upset and respond to me	3	2	1	0
I feel accepted and loved by my friends/family	3	2	1	0
The people close to me support me to do new things and make changes in my life	3	2	1	0
My mate accepts my sexuality	3	2	1	0
Those closest to me express caring and affection to me	3	2	1	0
I spend high-quality time with friends/family	3	2	1	0
I feel close and in touch with friends/family	3	2	1	0
I am able to give what I would like to my friends/family	3	2	1	0
I know that I am important to the people closest to me	3	2	1	0
I am honest with the people close to me and they are honest with me	3	2	1	0
I can ask for help from my family and friends when I need it	3	2	1	0
I can usually find people to "hang out" with	3	2	1	0
I know that others are there for me	3	2	1	0

40 ○

35 ○

27 ○

○

_____ + _____ + _____ + _____ = ○

Scale 6 Total

Perfor-mance Zone	4 Personal Changes	5 Personal Pressures	6 Personal Satisfac-tions
Optimal	○	○	○
Balance	○	○	○
Strain	○	○	○
Burnout	○	○	○

Once you have completed all 3 scales, darken the circle in each column of the sample StressMap® to the right that corresponds to the circle you darkened for each individual scale. The result will be a profile of your "personal" stress levels.

Source: Essi Systems, Inc., 126 South Park, San Francisco, CA 94107.

individual perception, and a physical reaction or response. Numerous factors can serve as stimuli for the stress response. Stressors can be real physiological or psychological factors, or they can be caused by anticipation, imagination, and emotions. Some common factors that cause stress are personality type, occupation, home life, college, major life events, and daily hassles. The next chapter examines the physical mechanisms of stress, focusing upon the physiological changes that the body experiences during the stress response. ᴡ

Stress and Physiology

I MAGINE an early American settler out hunting. It is a beautiful, sunny day with birds singing and wild flowers blooming. The settler is calm, relaxed, and truly enjoying himself. Suddenly, from a thicket some 50 yards away, he hears a loud noise and turns to see a bear charging. His body is immediately aroused either to fight or to run away from this enemy. He quickly cocks his rifle and fires but does so in such haste that he misses the charging bear. He considers holding his ground and using the rifle as a club; he considers attempting to outrun the animal; instead, he wisely chooses to climb a nearby tree.

The bear reaches the tree as the man is on the way up and slashes out with its giant paw. The sharp claws catch the settler on the left calf, causing several cuts, but, thanks to the enormous rush of energy caused by his stress response, he is able to continue on up the tree and out of the bear's reach. The huge bear growls and trudges around under the tree for several hours. Finally it tires and wanders off.

The stress response saved the settler's life, for it initiated specific bodily functions allowing him to escape. It caused the increased heart rate and blood pressure necessary to get blood to his muscle tissue, allowing him to run fast. It also quickened his respiration rate and allowed his lungs to hold more oxygen, which increased his stamina. Finally, it heightened his senses of sight, hearing, and smell to allow him to take in all of the events. It even caused the blood flowing from his leg wounds to clot more quickly than it would have in the absence of stress.

Our hunter experienced a typical "fight-or-flight" response. In this case, it was a totally appropriate response and probably saved his life. This chapter will look inside the human body to examine the physiology of the stress response and the toll it can take when it occurs inappropriately.

FIGURE 2.1
The Physical Responses to Stress

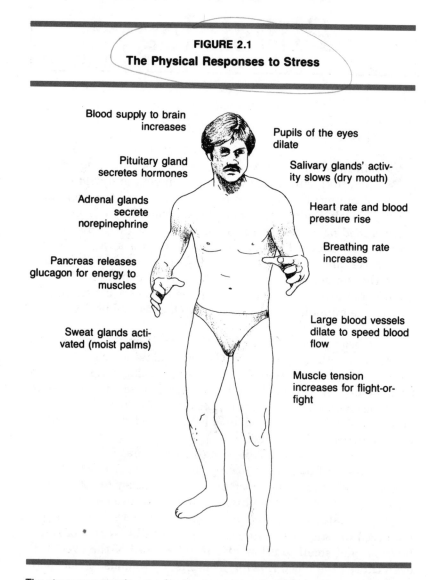

Blood supply to brain increases

Pituitary gland secretes hormones

Adrenal glands secrete norepinephrine

Pancreas releases glucagon for energy to muscles

Sweat glands activated (moist palms)

Pupils of the eyes dilate

Salivary glands' activity slows (dry mouth)

Heart rate and blood pressure rise

Breathing rate increases

Large blood vessels dilate to speed blood flow

Muscle tension increases for flight-or-fight

The stress response is nature's way of preparing the body for "fight or flight."

THE NERVOUS SYSTEM

Because the human stress response begins in the nervous system, it is important to understand the way in which this bodily function operates. The nervous system is divided into 2 main branches: the **central nervous system (CNS)** and the **peripheral nervous system (PNS)**. The CNS is composed of the brain and the spinal cord, and the PNS is composed of the remainder of the nerves throughout the body. These include the **somatic nervous system**, which carries sensory and motor signals to and from the CNS, and the **autonomic nervous system**, which carries the

FIGURE 2.2
The Nervous System

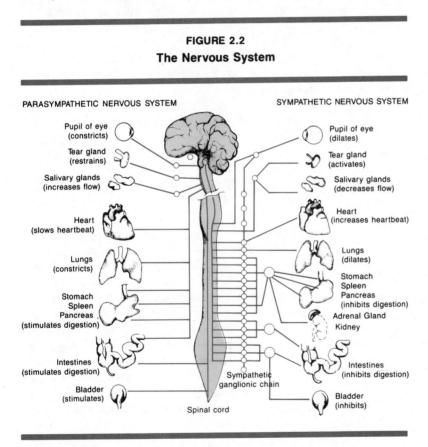

PARASYMPATHETIC NERVOUS SYSTEM   SYMPATHETIC NERVOUS SYSTEM

Pupil of eye (constricts)
Tear gland (restrains)
Salivary glands (increases flow)
Heart (slows heartbeat)
Lungs (constricts)
Stomach Spleen Pancreas (stimulates digestion)
Intestines (stimulates digestion)
Bladder (stimulates)
Spinal cord

Pupil of eye (dilates)
Tear gland (activates)
Salivary glands (decreases flow)
Heart (increases heartbeat)
Lungs (dilates)
Stomach Spleen Pancreas (inhibits digestion)
Adrenal Gland Kidney
Intestines (inhibits digestion)
Sympathetic ganglionic chain
Bladder (inhibits)

There are two divisions in the autonomic nervous system (ANS). The parasympathetic division predominates during quiet, restful periods and is involved in the normal regulation of organ systems. The sympathetic division is primarily active during periods of stress. The ANS connects the central nervous system to various parts of the body. The sympathetic and parasympathetic divisions continuously act in opposition to each other.

Central nervous system (CNS): The brain and the spinal cord.

Peripheral nervous system (PNS): The portion of the nervous system other than the brain and spinal cord.

Somatic nervous system: That portion of the peripheral nervous system that carries messages from the sense organs, and relays information that directs the voluntary movements of the skeletal muscles.

Autonomic nervous system (ANS): The portion of the nervous system that carries messages from the central nervous system to the endocrine glands, the smooth muscles controlling the heart, and the involuntary muscles; includes both the sympathetic and parasympathetic nervous systems.

Sympathetic nervous system: The part of the nervous system that carries stimulating neural signals.

Parasympathetic nervous system: The part of the nervous system that carries calming neural signals.

Cognitive: The higher mental activities–perceiving, thinking, and knowing.

Neurons: The impulse-conducting cells that are the functioning units of the nervous system; nerve cells.

Adrenal medulla: The core of the adrenal gland; it produces adrenaline and noradrenaline.

Catecholamines: Hormones, including adrenaline and noradrenaline, that are released into the bloodstream by the adrenal glands as part of the stress response, to stimulate the body and prepare it for action.

Adrenaline: A hormone produced in the adrenal medulla that helps control the speed of the heart rate and the strength of the heartbeat, and alerts the body for action in times of stress. Also called epinephrine.

Noradrenaline: A hormone produced in the adrenal medulla causes blood vessels to contract when blood pressure gets too low. Often the release of noradrenaline is triggered by stress. Also called norepinephrine.

impulses that regulate the body's internal functioning, such as heart rate or respiration.

The system of autonomic nerves can be further divided into the **sympathetic nervous system** and the **parasympathetic nervous system**. The sympathetic nervous system carries signals that stimulate the body and prepare it for action. The parasympathetic nervous system does the opposite, calming the body down.

THE HUMAN STRESS RESPONSE

The stress response begins when a signal stimulates the sensory receptors of the PNS. Impulses are then sent from the sensory receptors to the brain. Within the brain, emotions are integrated with higher level **cognitive**, or rational thinking, functions, so that the individual is able to interpret whether the original signal is indeed threatening.

If the brain decides that the signal does not represent a threat, no further response takes place. If, however, it is perceived as a threat (a stressor), the stress response will proceed. In the final analysis, the stress response results from both the cognitive interpretation of a stimulus and the associated emotional arousal, rather than from the stimulus alone. In other words, it is the individual's perception of the event that ultimately determines a stress response.

Once an event is perceived as threatening, the sympathetic branch of the autonomic nervous system sends electrical impulses directly to the heart, muscles, and respiratory system. Heart rate, blood pressure, muscle tension, and respiration increase, while digestion and kidney function decrease. The effects are temporary, however, because the **neurons** (nerve cells) can carry only a limited number of impulses to the affected organs.

If direct nerve stimulation were the only way to create a state of arousal, the stress response would be short-lived. Fortunately, this is not the case. While the sympathetic nerves are stimulating various organs to create the initial response, they are also signaling the **adrenal medulla** to release **catecholamines** (**adrenaline** and **noradrenaline**). The catecholamines, particularly adrenaline, produce an effect identical to that produced by direct nervous system stimulation except that it starts 20 to 30 seconds later and lasts 10 times longer. Therefore, by the time the direct neural impulses weaken, the adrenaline is already present and maintaining the increased level of arousal needed to confront the stressor.

But the process is not yet through. The elements of the endocrine system now begin their slow but prolonged response. Neural impulses stimulate the hypothalamus (located in the brain) to release **corticotropin-releasing factor (CRF)**. The CRF stimulates the pituitary gland to release **adrenocorticotropic hormone (ACTH)**. ACTH then acts upon the adrenal glands, causing them to continue releasing the catecholamines and to release the **glucocorticoids** (cortisol, or hydrocortisone, and corticosterone). Among other things, the glucocorticoids increase glucose production, thus helping to maintain the increased energy levels needed to cope with a stressor. [1] As the body tries to maintain its heightened state of arousal, many more hormones are released and other body systems are affected. In essence, every system in the human body is affected by the stress response.

Now we can see more clearly how our settler friend survived. In today's world, we are seldom chased by wild bears, but there are still times when the fight-or-flight response is appropriate: if a prowler breaks into our house, for instance, or if we are confronted by a barking dog while jogging.

But, as mentioned in chapter 1, the stressors we are most likely to encounter today are not usually life-threatening and do not require the physical adaptations associated with fight-or-flight; for instance, an argument with a spouse or a missed deadline. Our bodies automatically react with the fight-or-flight response even though it is not appropriate or even possible physically to fight or run away. Our bodies are primed for physical action but have no opportunity to take action. Over time, this constant state of arousal can lead to exhaustion or a host of stress-related diseases and maladies.

STRESS AND DISEASE

Stress is related to many types of diseases. Some people theorize, in fact, that every disease is either directly or indirectly related to stress. Certainly much more research needs to be conducted before such a statement can be substantiated, but given what is now known, the possibility of such a relationship cannot be totally discounted.

In some instances, a prolonged stress reaction may actually cause a disease such as ulcers. In other instances, prolonged stress may wear natural resistance down and make people more susceptible to the disease process. In either case, if stress had been controlled, the condition might have been avoided. Let us

(continued on p. 37)

Corticotropin-releasing factor (CRF): A chemical released by the hypothalamus that causes the pituitary to secrete adrenocorticotropic hormone (ACTH).

Adrenocorticotropic hormone (ACTH): A hormone, secreted by the pituitary gland, that acts on the adrenal cortex, stimulating growth and secretion of corticosteroids, including glucocorticoids. The production of ACTH is increased during times of stress. Also known as corticotropin.

Glucocorticoids: The hormones cortisol and corticosterone, which are released from the adrenal glands and influence fat, carbohydrate, and protein metabolism. This includes increasing glucose production, thus helping to maintain the increased energy needs associated with a stress response.

The Crippling Ills That Stress Can Trigger

Jim, a soft-spoken, 45-year-old financial analyst, is all too familiar with the effects of stress in the workplace. When his organization was plagued by layoffs and cutbacks, he began to act "bizarrely," he says. Jim's mood swings eventually put off his managers. As a result, he was demoted to a department that was less visible and where his skills were ill-suited to the job.

It took seven years before Jim's ailment was correctly diagnosed. He is one of 10 million Americans who suffer from depression serious enough to warrant medical attention. Jim believes that his illness—bipolar, or manic, depression—was triggered by his failure to cope with job-related stress.

EARLY WARNINGS. Doctors agree that when stress is left untreated it can lead to more serious mood disorders such as depression and anxiety—especially among those with a genetic predisposition to such ailments. That's because stress and depression share a common chemistry in the brain. A hormone called corticotropin-releasing hormone (CRH) marshals the body's defenses against stress. Even after the stress subsides, the body keeps releasing the hormone, sometimes for years. CRH is also found in elevated levels in the brains of people who suffer from depression. That helps explain why depression recurs and why each new episode increases the chances of a recurrence.

This makes it particularly important to deal with stress on the job while it's still at a manageable level. The symptoms may be physical, psychological, or both. Early warning signs such as headaches, back pain, irritability, insomnia, absenteeism from work, overeating, and heavy drinking are all too easy to dismiss. But they can lead to serious emotional disorders as well as aggravate ulcers and heart disease.

Whether stress will escalate into something more serious seems to depend on a number of factors, including the severity and duration of the stress and the individual's ability to cope. "It's the frame of mind that's important rather than the stressful event itself," says Alan Breier, clinical

director of the out-patient program at the Maryland Psychiatric Research Center in Catonsville, Md. "What matters is whether the stress leaves a person feeling helpless and out of control."

When stress gets out of hand, the most serious consequence—severe depression—often goes untreated. Typically, only about 10% of depression sufferers get the medical help they need. That failure can be fatal: Depressed individuals make up some 60% of all suicides. A major problem is misdiagnosis. Biochemical tests can distinguish between certain kinds of mood disorders, however they are often unreliable.

'LIKE A FEVER.' So most doctors rely on a complicated checklist of psychological symptoms. Diagnosis is tricky because many mood disorders have similar manifestations. Bipolar depression, for example, is often mistaken for schizophrenia—especially during the manic, rather than the depressive, phase of the disease. And mood disorders also produce symptoms that mimic those of about 75 different physical problems, such as drug poisoning, a malfunctioning thyroid gland, or multiple sclerosis. "Depression is like a fever," says Dr. William Z. Potter, a neuropharmacologist at the National Institutes of Mental Health. "It's a nonspecific response of the brain to a variety of environmental and metabolic stresses."

Anxiety can also be hard to spot. Its early signs are similar to those of stress, but it can escalate into the debilitating unfocused fear known as panic attacks, heart palpitations, or hot and cold flashes. "During normal stress, we can pinpoint the things that we're aroused about, whether they are the demands of jobs and marriages or whatever," says Dr. Steven M. Paul, chief of the clinical neuroscience branch of the NIMH. "But with anxiety we can't say exactly why we're disturbed."

When full-blown depression does develop, it usually casts an umbrella of long-lasting symptoms. It may manifest itself as sadness, but sufferers often say they simply feel "dulled," incapable of carrying out even the simplest task.

It can also be seasonal: One form afflicts people in the winter, another—more difficult to treat—in the summer.

An ongoing inexplicable sadness may also be caused by a little understood condition called dysthymic disorder (DD). This condition, which afflicts an estimated 5 million Americans, mostly women, causes sufferers to have "the blues" most of the time—but usually not enough to seek help. While depression can subside in six months if untreated, DD persists for at least two years.

EYE OF THE BEHOLDER. Many doctors prescribe drugs to attack DD and depression. But psychotherapy, particularly such short-term forms as cognitive behavior therapy, can also be highly effective, especially when used to treat milder forms of depression or DD. In very severe cases, once-discredited shock therapy can often help. For some forms of depression, sleep deprivation or light treatments also work.

But it's much easier to deal with stress before it becomes serious. A handful of companies, such as IBM, AT&T, Xerox, and Johnson & Johnson, have set up model programs that include every-thing from exercise and meditation to counseling and referrals.

Denis B. Woodfield, director of corporate treasury services for Johnson & Johnson, is one who believes they help. His reaction to stress was eating—and eating. His 6-foot, 1-inch frame ballooned to 300 pounds, and he developed a bleeding ulcer. Three years ago he joined J&J's wellness program. Its regimen of exercise and dieting pared 75 pounds. "It clears my mind so that I feel better," he says.

To some extent, stress is in the eye of the beholder—the difference between perceiving the weather as partly sunny or partly cloudy. Keeping a balance between work, family, and cultural, intellectual, or athletic interests helps one manage stress. The best defense may be a positive attitude, welcoming change and pressure as challenges—not threats.

—*Sana Siwolop in New York, with Reginald Rhein Jr. in Washington and Joe Weber in Philadelphia*

Source: *Business Week*, 18 April 1988, p. 77.

now look at some specific illnesses or illness-related conditions that have been linked to stress.

Immune Dysfunction

The immune system is perhaps one of the most sophisticated systems of the body. Its primary function is to provide immunity to disease. **Immunity** is the ability to overcome the effects of a particular disease-causing agent (such as a virus) and thus prevent or fight off infection. As might be expected, the effects of stress on this highly developed system are complex and involve a wide range of neurobiological mechanisms. Initial studies have demonstrated that stressful conditions can profoundly suppress the immune responses of the blood and **lymphocytes**. [2]

Two of the many types of cells produced by the immune system are **T-cells** (thymus-derived cells) and **B-cells** (bone-marrow-derived cells). T-cells fight bacterial infections, some viral infections, and fungal infections; they also combat cancer cells. B-cells neutralize foreign agents.

Immunity: Protection against infectious diseases provided by the body's immune system and acquired through immunization, previous infection, or genetic predisposition.

Lymphocytes: White blood cells that participate in the body's immune reaction to infections.

T-cells: Lymphocytes produced in the thymus gland that govern cellular immunity and assist the B-cells in producing antibodies.

B-cells: Lymphocytes produced in the bone marrow that attack foreign agents in the blood or other bodily fluids.

(continued on p. 39)

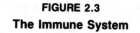

FIGURE 2.3
The Immune System

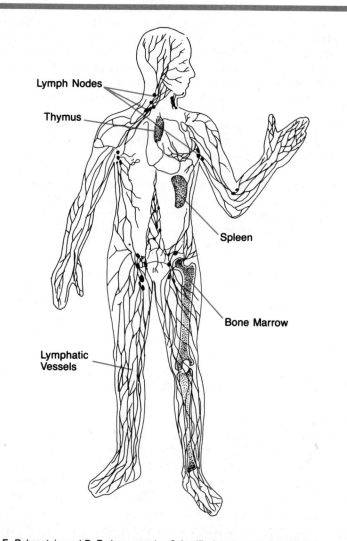

Source: E. Rubenstein and D. Federman, eds., *Scientific American Medicine* (1987).

The immune system is the body's natural defense against infectious disease. Its primary weapons are the antibodies produced and carried to the site of the invasion of the disease-fighting white blood cells known as lymphocytes. These cells, produced in the bone marrow, thymus, and spleen, are concentrated in the lymph nodes and transported throughout the body by the lymphatic vessels and bloodstream.

During a stress response, the immune system is initially stimulated to increase its activity. At the same time, however, some hormones produced by the stress response (particularly cortisol) tend to suppress or damage both T-cells and B-cells. As a result, resistance to many infectious diseases declines and the individual may be more susceptible to a variety of common ailments, such as colds or flu. In addition, exposure to long periods of stress may increase some people's susceptibility to serious **chronic disorders**, perhaps even cancer. [3]

Did You Know That . . .

A recent study showed that people in cognitive therapy who were learning to change self-defeating beliefs developed more "killer cells" in their immune systems.

Stress's Effect on Immune System

Researchers at Ohio State University have shown that relatively minor stress—the kind medical students may feel during final exams, for example—seems to interfere with important genetic messages that help control the immune system. It may be the first time that anyone has connected stress with gene expression. "We're really getting down to the nitty-gritty mechanisms," says Ronald Glaser, professor of medical microbiology and immunology, "and not just broadly saying 'stress affects immunity.' "

The work lends additional support to the growing field of psychoneuroimmunology, which proposes that stress and loneliness leave people vulnerable to disease. Research in recent years, much of it by Glaser and Ohio State psychologist Janice Kiecolt-Glaser, has shown that a variety of stressful situations—the death of a parent or close friend, a poor marriage, even keeping emotions bottled up inside—can weaken a person's immune response.

Glaser explains that, when people are under duress, T-lymphocytes (white blood cells that are among the main line of defense to infection) don't respond as well as usual to attack by bacteria and viruses. He and his colleagues studied lymphokines, potent chemicals such as certain types of interferon and interleukin-2 (IL-2) that rev up the immune system, launching lymphocytes in particular.

Previously, they saw that gamma interferon activity fell off in people under stress. With this in mind, they compared the illness-fighting capabilities of a group of medical students before and during final exams. They measured a number of factors, among them the presence of IL-2 receptors—chemical docking sites—on lymphocytes. These receptors allow the **interleukin** molecule to hook on to the white blood cells, sending them into action. The researchers found fewer available receptors in the exam-taking students than in the non-stressed group.

The next step was to see how far, cellularly, the effects of stress might actually go. Glaser and his co-workers delved into the genetic

Chronic disorders: Disorders that persist over a long period of time.

Interleukin: A group of protein factors that act as a messenger between white blood cells involved in immune responses.

material of the cell to see whether its blueprint for constructing the interleukin receptors was affected.

"All of this tells us that stress is doing something to hinder cell function," Glaser reports. "We've now been able to show a direct effect of stress on gene expression for one of these cell receptors for an important immune system activator—IL-2—that's required for T-cell functioning. It's all consistent with what we've seen: T-lymphocytes—and the immune system—don't work as well under stress."

However, he still isn't sure what the results say about the effects of stress on health risk and disease. "The field now has gone on beyond simply making observations. We have to find out why these immune system changes are happening and what the health implications are. We've just found a few more pieces of the puzzle."

Source: *USA Today*, June 1989, p. 4.

Allergies, Chronic Muscle Tension, and Ulcers

Allergies occur when the body's immune system mistakes a harmless substance for one it perceives as threatening. Because stress affects the immunological response of the body, allergies can be stress-related. [4] For example, children with some forms of asthma that are triggered by an allergic reaction often suffer attacks after experiencing physical or emotional stress.

The chronic muscle tension that is often associated with an intense or prolonged stress response can bring about tension headaches, migraine headaches, and backaches. Ulcers, which are open sores in the lining of the stomach, can result from an increase in digestive juices associated with prolonged stress. [5] Other problems affecting the digestive system that are associated with stress include diarrhea caused by an overworking colon and constipation caused by an underworking colon. [6]

Stress and the Cardiovascular System

Hypertension (high blood pressure) is a known risk factor for heart disease, particularly when it is sustained over time. Stress can cause an immediate rise in blood pressure. Normally this increase will last only a few hours, but chronic stress may lead to persistent hypertension. [7] It must be remembered that stress is only one of several risk factors for hypertension; others include smoking and excessive alcohol consumption. Ironically, people often use smoking and drinking as methods of coping with stress. Therefore, it is possible that stress and inappropriate stress-control measures together can cause hypertension. In any case,

(continued on p. 43)

FIGURE 2.4
Allergies and Stress

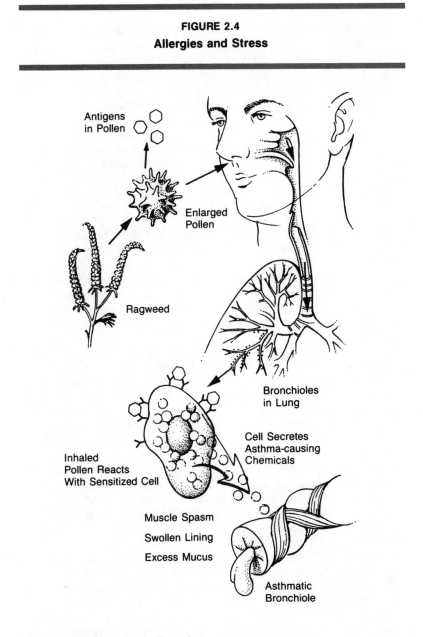

Antigens
in Pollen

Enlarged
Pollen

Ragweed

Bronchioles
in Lung

Cell Secretes
Asthma-causing
Chemicals

Inhaled
Pollen Reacts
With Sensitized Cell

Muscle Spasm

Swollen Lining

Excess Mucus

Asthmatic
Bronchiole

Source: Leonard Dank, Medical Illustrations.

Allergies occur when the body's immune system mistakes a harmless substance for one it perceives as threatening. Some allergic reactions, including some forms of asthma, can be stress-related.

Although the management of stress-related stomach ulcers has advanced considerably, their cause remains largely undetermined. Now, research from the University of Southern California offers new evidence that the ulcers originate in the brain, not the stomach. USC scientists have identified the lower brain stem as the site of the action of a hormone known to stimulate gastric acid secretion and induce stomach ulcers.

Ulcers: Brain May Be the Villain

The brain stem, located between the spinal cord and the brain, most frequently is associated with maintaining circulation, breathing, and other vital body functions. The researchers found that an area in the brain stem of laboratory rats is particularly sensitive to the ulcerogenic effects of the brain chemical TRH (thyrotropin-releasing hormone). Other areas were tested, but did not show this sensitivity.

Knowing this site of action could help in diagnosis, says Daniel Hernandez, associate professor of research medicine at the USC School of Medicine. For example, alteration of the lower brain stem through trauma or a tumor could explain why certain ulcers form. At a more basic level, the discovery could help explain the origins of peptic ulcer disease, particularly the mechanisms for gastric ulcers caused by stress.

"Evidence that the brain is involved in producing stress ulcers has existed for more than 200 years. But the specifics as to how they're formed or the mechanisms involved in the onset have remained elusive." Stress ulcers frequently are associated with trauma to the central nervous system, malignant diseases, organ failure, or psychological stress. In these ulcers, a sore forms in the stomach wall, extending through the mucous lining and penetrating underlying tissue.

Ulcers can bleed and, with massive bleeding, can be fatal. Treatment includes drugs that inhibit the production of gastric acid, which eats away at the mucous lining, or antacids that form a protective coating over the ulcer, allowing it to heal. A surgical treatment is to sever the vagus nerve, which originates in the brain stem and stimulates gastric acid production.

Why does stress cause ulcers? Hernandez has pursued the question by focusing on the central nervous system and the pathways connecting the brain to the gastrointestinal tract. In laboratory rats, he has found hormones in the adrenal gland that are regulated by the brain and exert protection against stress-induced ulcers. "It appears that the coping response to stress is initiated centrally in the brain and that chemical messages are sent out to the peripheral organs of the endocrine system, causing the release of stress-related hormones. These hormones, in turn, act on specific receptors in the stomach that protect the gastric mucosa from the damaging effects of stress. So the brain is pivotal in initiating a cascade of events."

Identifying the lower brain stem as the site of action for the ulcerogenic effects of TRH is significant since the lower brain stem is where the vagus nerve originates. "The puzzle isn't solved yet, but we're shedding light on the specific brain chemicals and structures that may explain the onset of stress gastric ulcers. Perhaps someday a synthetic analog of TRH . . . will be developed. . . ."

Source: *USA Today,* February 1989, p. 16

Did You Know That . . .

Doctors believe some cases of sudden cardiac arrest, which kills 400,000 people a year, are caused by stress, which induces wildly erratic heart rhythms.

there is evidence that proper stress management can lower blood pressure. [8]

Stress also affects other aspects of the cardiovascular system. Studies have shown that stress can lead to heart **arrhythmias** and, in particular, to **tachycardia** (accelerated heart rate) [9], which can be fatal if left untreated. Evidence indicates that catecholamines released during the stress response can have damaging effects on the heart. Animal studies have demonstrated that psychological stress induces myocardial damage, hypertension, vascular changes, and can increase the risk of sudden cardiac death. Medical literature and the clinical observations of many physicians include numerous reports of sudden cardiac deaths that, in all probability, were induced or hastened by stressful life experiences. [10]

Stroke, another potential consequence of the stress response, can occur if hypertension is left untreated. A stroke results from a leak or interruption in the brain's blood supply, which can in turn be caused by a ruptured blood vessel in the brain. A sudden stress reaction with increased blood pressure could result in such a rupture, particularly at a site where the blood vessel was already weakened.

Stress and Cancer

The relationship between stress and cancer is intriguing and remains somewhat mysterious. Some researchers have attempted to identify personality traits that may predispose some people to cancer. Although these studies are not definitive, some association has been found between cancer and some personality characteristics, including impaired self-awareness, impaired introspective capacity, pent-up emotions, repressed aggression, and a predisposition for experiencing hopelessness and despair. [11]

Available data does not support the conclusion that stress acts directly as a **carcinogen**. That is, stress does not directly cause cancer. It may, however, weaken the resistance of the body

Arrhythmias: Any variation from a normal heartbeat.

Tachycardia: Abnormally fast heart rate.

Carcinogen: Any substance known to cause cancer.

(continued on p. 45)

Without so much as a single chest pain, more than a quarter of a million people die each year from heart attacks. What they don't feel can obviously hurt them, and several British researchers believe that stress may mask pain that would provide a valuable sign of heart trouble.

When blood does not circulate adequately to the heart—a condition called myocardial **ischemia**—some people experience chest pain. Ischemia, however, can also occur without causing pain. Both painful and "silent" episodes of ischemia have been linked to psychological stress, so cardiologist Leisa J. Freeman and colleagues decided to explore the connection between the two.

Stress and the Silent Heart Attack

The researchers monitored the heart function of 30 patients during a potentially stressful period while they waited to find out if they needed bypass surgery, and again after they had adjusted to the treatment decision. During both 48-hour periods, these patients recorded all episodes of chest pain, what they were doing at the time and any feelings of emotional upset. The researchers also measured patients' anxiety and depression as well as levels of certain stress hormones in their urine.

Freeman and colleagues found that pain accompanied episodes of restricted blood flow only one-third of the time. A majority of the patients experienced more "silent" episodes before their course of treatment had been decided upon than they did afterward. These patients also mentioned more feelings of upset during the stressful period, and they generally had higher levels of anxiety and depression. Stress hormone levels further supported the link between the absence of pain and the presence of stress: As levels of these hormones in the patient's urine increased, so did episodes of silent ischemia.

Freeman and colleagues suggest that reduced blood flow to the heart produces pain mainly in response to activities, such as taking a walk. Silent ischemia, in contrast, may be the cardiovascular system's way of reacting to a more sustained influence, such as stress.

The researchers also suggest that stress may actually mask people's perception of pain or divert their attention away from it. Like the marathoner who runs the final mile of a race on bloody feet, perhaps "the patient ignores or dismisses as trivial the pain . . . [when] under psychological stress."

—*Marjory Roberts*

Source: *Psychology Today,* August 1987, p. 7.

Ischemia: Inadequate blood supply to an organ, resulting in a disruption of normal function.

FIGURE 2.5
Symptoms and Risk Factors of Stroke

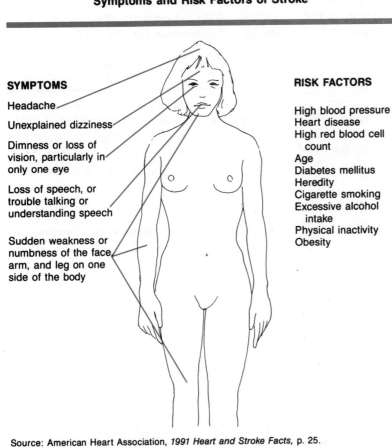

SYMPTOMS

Headache

Unexplained dizziness

Dimness or loss of
vision, particularly in
only one eye

Loss of speech, or
trouble talking or
understanding speech

Sudden weakness or
numbness of the face,
arm, and leg on one
side of the body

RISK FACTORS

High blood pressure
Heart disease
High red blood cell
    count
Age
Diabetes mellitus
Heredity
Cigarette smoking
Excessive alcohol
    intake
Physical inactivity
Obesity

Source: American Heart Association, *1991 Heart and Stroke Facts*, p. 25.

Some stroke risk factors are the result of heredity or natural processes and are
beyond our control. Others, such as cigarette smoking, excessive alcohol intake, and
physical inactivity, can be modified through changes in life-style.

and allow direct-acting carcinogens, such as the by-products of
cigarette combustion, to take hold. In addition, since stress
affects both hormonal and immunological functioning, it could
contribute to the spreading (metastasis) of a cancerous tumor
from its original location to additional sites in the body, but this
has not been documented.

In summary, there is no known cause-and-effect relationship between stress and cancer. It would seem certain, however, that any cancer diagnosis is itself a stress-causing occurrence and that the profound physiological effects caused by prolonged stress may influence the development of cancerous tumors. [12]

TEMPOROMANDIBULAR JOINT SYDROME (TMJ)

A relative newcomer to the list of stress-related diseases and disorders is TMJ, or **temporomandibular joint syndrome**. TMJ is an irritation of the joint connecting the jawbone and skull and is characterized by severe toothaches, ear and neck aches, head-

FIGURE 2.6

TMJ

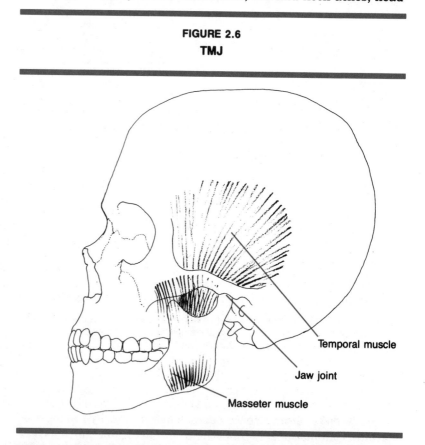

Temporal muscle

Jaw joint

Masseter muscle

Temporomandibular joint syndrome (TMJ): A disorder characterized by inflammation of the muscles, nerves, and tissues that surround the jaw joints.

Temporomandibular joint syndrome (TMJ) is indicated by pain and other symptoms affecting the head, jaw, and face that are believed to result when the temporomandibular joints (jaw joints) and the muscles and ligaments that control and support them do not work together correctly. The condition may be triggered by clenching or grinding the teeth.

aches, and a locking or clicking of the jaw. The American Dental Association estimates that about 10 million Americans suffer from some form of TMJ. TMJ can be caused by physical traumas such as car accidents and faulty dental work. It can also result from stress. Typically, people who clench or grind their teeth in response to stress are more vulnerable.

Patients with mild cases of stress-caused TMJ may respond to relaxation exercises. More severe cases may require a bite plate to prevent teeth-grinding or anti-inflammatory drugs to reduce the swelling and pain. As a last resort, surgery may be needed to restore proper jaw movement. [13]

TMJ: When Teeth Bite Back

You're about to begin an important presentation that could mean a hefty percentage of next year's revenue. Just as you take your place near the flip chart, your pesky tooth flares up again.

This isn't the mere chilly thrill of a pinprick cavity. This is compounded punishment for life's little transgressions—for canceling dental appointments, for the times you didn't floss, for eating those little chocolates you found on hotel pillows. As you stand before all those people who surely have perfect, pain-free teeth, you just know that you're in for a root canal.

But your dentist may not find any decay. It may be that during the night you have been working out your stresses, and your teeth are finally telling you to knock it off. As you sleep, you may be clenching and grinding your teeth, putting heavy stress on your nerve endings, jaw, and joints. The painful result is called temporomandibular joint syndrome, or simply TMJ. It is an inflammation of the muscles, tissues, and nerve endings where the jaw is hinged to the skull. In addition to severe toothaches, TMJ symptoms also include a clicking jaw, neck and ear aches, tension headaches, even sinus problems.

For clothing retailer Jerry Goldberg, the pain was so sudden and severe that his wife thought he was suffering a stroke. "My pain went into my ears and head. It just drove me crazy," says the Jenkintown, Pa., owner of Boytogs-Upperclass-man Inc., a clothing store for men and boys.

His dentist referred him to a root-canal specialist, who in turn referred him to Neil Gottehrer, a dentist and director of the Craniofacial Pain Center in Abington, Pa. With his fingers, Gottehrer applied pressure on the muscles and nerve endings in Goldberg's jaw. That gave Goldberg relief that lasted several days, long enough for him to catch up on his sleep and for Gottehrer to build Goldberg a bite plate—an acrylic mouthpiece that would inhibit his constant clenching of his teeth. "Since then I've had no problems at all," he says. "I don't have to use my bite plate during the day, which I did for the first couple of weeks."

The American Dental Association says about 10 million Americans suffer from some form of TMJ. The syndrome is usually caused by traumas such as car accidents, faulty dental work that affects the bite, and stress. Gottehrer sees TMJ cases relatively evenly distributed among all three causes.

Big-city generalist dentists tell a different story, however. "About 95 percent of my cases are stress-related, and working people with high responsibility are common candidates for TMJ treatment," says David Rothkopf, a Washington dentist and a former TMJ patient himself. "We all have stress, and something might tip it off. The temporomandibular joint becomes a target organ to vent nervous energy."

Because the symptoms usually first appear in the teeth, dentists are more likely to know about and diagnose TMJ. However, since the problem area is where the jaw meets the skull, it's an orthopedic condition—the physician's jurisdiction. Moreover, if the problem is caused by stress, some psychotherapy may be called for during treatment. As a result of all the health-care specialties involved, and because the bite plate is considered an orthopedic appliance, TMJ treatment is usually covered under medical insurance—a plus for those in small businesses that can't afford dental insurance for employees.

If stress-caused TMJ is treated early, says Rothkopf, it's possible that the patient can be treated with relaxing exercises. More advanced cases require mild tranquilizers for starters and a bite plate, which can cost between $400 and $800. Rothkopf also advises that TMJ has become a fashionable diagnosis among the professions, and that it's possible to diagnose TMJ when a root canal really is necessary. But, he says, when a root canal diagnosis is uncertain and TMJ is a possibility, it's better to try treating for TMJ first.

Gottehrer agrees: "Whatever treatment is the least invasive and offers the greatest amount of relief is the best approach. There has been an excessive amount of expense and unnecessary surgery for misdiagnosed patients."

—*Martha I. Finney*

Source: *Nation's Business,* March 1989, p. 65.

Blindness

A particular form of blindness, **central serous chorioretinopathy (CSC)**, has been related to high levels of stress. Researchers speculate that during periods of high stress, elevated blood pressure and the presence of certain hormones can damage small blood vessels near the retina of the eye. When these blood vessels leak, the structure that attaches the retina to the eye weakens, which can eventually result in a detachment of the retina. When this occurs, the victim becomes blind in that eye. Fortunately, laser surgery can correct CSC. If the patient does not learn to manage his or her stress, however, relapse is likely. [14]

SUMMARY

The stress response occurs whenever we perceive a given stimulus as threatening. This process begins with neural stimulation of the end organs in preparation for fight or flight and soon involves every major system of the body. Although these actions are normal and necessary if caused by a true physical stressor, they are inappropriate for the type of stress most people face in today's society.

Over time, chronic stress can play a role in the development of a variety of diseases. In some situations, changes brought about by the stress response itself cause the disease. In others, the stress response wears down the body's immune system and allows diseases to take hold. Stress has been linked to everything from toothaches and blindness to cancer and heart disease.

Central serous chorioretinopathy: A form of blindness that can be caused by a stress response; it results when elevated blood pressure and the presence of certain hormones damage blood vessels near the retina of the eye.

She was 32 years old and happily married—or so she thought. But then her bubble of bliss burst. Her husband suddenly left her, and she spent hours listening to the songs they used to dance to, submerged in memories of an existence run afoul. But she really hit rock bottom the day she woke up partially blind.

Did our heroine suffer from an acute case of Patsy Clineitis? Not

She's Got the Blinding Blues

exactly. She was a victim of *central serous chorioretinopathy* (CSC), a stress-induced weakening of the retina resulting in blindness in one eye.

A new study of 33 patients with vision loss has confirmed that stress was a factor in 30 of those examined. According to head researchers Gary S. Gelber, MD, assistant clinical professor of psychiatry at the University of California, San Francisco (UCSF), and Howard Schatz, MD, clinical professor of ophthalmology at UCSF, the patients experienced a stressful event weeks or even hours before they lost their vision. What's more, 97 percent of the patients qualified as hard-driving type A perfectionists.

Why does stress affect the eyes? The researchers speculate that the effects of stress—soaring blood pressure and a release of "fight or flight" hormones—injure the blood vessels near the retina. When these vessels and capillaries around the retina leak, the structure that attaches the retina to the eye weakens, gradually resulting in blindness. In severe cases, the retina eventually totally detaches. Fortunately, the condition is reversible if the person can get over his or her source of stress. CSC can also be corrected by such methods as laser surgery.

Though Drs. Gelber and Schatz are the first researchers to thoroughly examine the emotional basis for central serous chorioretinopathy, this disorder isn't quite as obscure as it sounds. However, since doctors are just beginning to understand its causes and effects, its victims often go undiagnosed. Gelber and Schatz have found that most of their patients are under 50 years of age.

—*Devera Pine*

Source: *Health,* January 1988, p. 20.

Did You Know That . . .

In one study, over 90 percent of people with detached retinas had experienced one or more very stressful events just before developing the eye disorder.

Thus far this book has considered the bad news about stress. The good news is that people can learn to manage this aspect of life quite effectively and even put that energy to use for their benefit. The remaining chapters will present an overview of a comprehensive approach to stress management and examine a variety of stress reduction/stress control techniques. W

C H A P T E R

3

Managing Stress: An Overview

MODERATE AMOUNTS OF STRESS are not only desirable but necessary. Stress can motivate us to attain desirable goals, such as college degrees, professional recognition, job promotions, and even tangible items, such as automobiles and new homes. Studies on productive and creative peaks point out that we respond best not when our stress level is low, but when it is close to the threshold of what we can stand. [1]

The psychiatrist A. H. Lockwood uncovered this stress-performance relationship in a study of musicians. He noted that a certain amount of stress may help those whose professional standings depend upon public performance, because it serves as a motivating force and helps focus attention. Lockwood also found, however, that excessive levels of stress are clearly detrimental and may lead to **performance anxiety**. Also known as stage fright, performance anxiety is a syndrome characterized by nervousness, fear, tremors, tachycardia, shortness of breath, sweaty palms, dry mouth, nausea, and an urge to urinate. In other words, once the optimal level of stress is passed, performance and the overall quality of life deteriorate rapidly. The goal of stress management is not to eliminate stress but to learn to control and use it to its best advantage.

None of this is easy. It is often difficult to balance all of life's demands, many of which are uncontrollable. Managing stress successfully requires true commitment because it may entail developing not only new skills but new life-style habits.

Performance anxiety: A stress-related syndrome, characterized by a fear of performing before an audience, that produces pronounced symptoms of anxiety; particularly severe cases may result in an inability to perform.

50

FIGURE 3.1
Goal of Stress Management

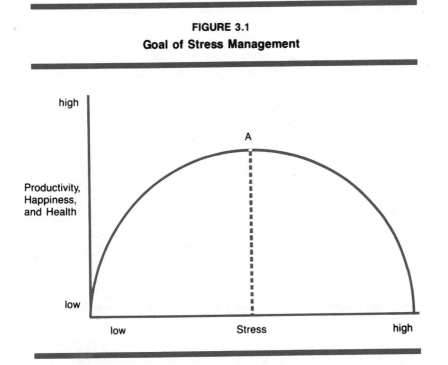

The goal of stress management is not to eliminate stress completely but to control it and use it to its best advantage.

COMPREHENSIVE AND INDIVIDUAL PROGRAMS

A stress-management program must be comprehensive. Most stressful situations involve 3 elements: a stressor, a perception of stress, and a physical and emotional reaction. **Comprehensive stress management** requires controlling all 3 of these elements.

From a practical perspective this involves techniques designed to eliminate, modify, or control stressors; to alter individual perceptions of stressors; and to manage or control the stress response once it occurs. By learning and practicing these techniques, one can learn to manage stress so that it does not become detrimental to happiness, productivity, or health.

In addition to being comprehensive, stress-management programs must also be personalized. The tools required to manage stress effectively differ from person to person. Judy, for example,

Comprehensive stress management: A stress-management approach that involves controlling the 3 elements that cause a stress response: the stressor, the perception of stress by the individual, and the physical and emotional reaction to stress.

has so many activities going on in her life that she is always hurrying. She finds it difficult to say no to others and has poor time-management skills. John, on the other hand, usually has his stressors under control, but his personality and perception of events cause him much stress. He is overly competitive, too aggressive in his personal interactions, and has a poor self-concept. Jill manages stressors most of the time and has few perception problems, but when unavoidable stress occurs, she does not know how to handle it well.

Although all 3 of these people need a comprehensive stress-management program, each has problems that obviously need individual attention. Personalized programs are also important because people react differently to intervention techniques. For example, some people find meditation highly attractive, whereas others may associate it with the practice of Far Eastern religions, which does not appeal to them. If meditation is the only stress-

(continued on p. 55)

A New View of Stress

If the health movement of the 1980s had a buzz-word, it was stress. Terms such as worry, anxiety, fear, impatience, and anger gave way to stress and its offshoots (stressful, stress-related, and stressed-out). Commentators spoke of the "age of stress," and speculated on stress as a factor in illness and other adverse events of life. And, certainly, scientific researchers led the chorus, as study after study on the subject made it into print. Is stress really the phantom killer of modern times?

According to Professor Leonard Syme of the University of California at Berkeley, it's time the psychological concept of stress—as something originating in a person's mind—was retired. Stress has never had an adequate definition, beyond such vague generalizations as "stress is how people respond to demands." "Stressors" have been defined as everything from wars and famine to job loss, family arguments, and encounters with the IRS. Further complicating matters is the fact that different people react to the same "stress" in unpredictable ways. The idea that personality flaws are at the bottom of stress-related illnesses has simply not been proven. It's been hard to demonstrate that specific attitudes lead to specific illnesses.

Indeed, the idea that emotional anguish arises from personality or individual wrongheadedness beclouds the fact that many physical and psychological problems come from social conditions not always within an individual's control. Many problems arise specifically from a person's occupation and financial situation. (Not having a job at all can be at least as painful as having the wrong one.) Of course, the workplace is not the only source of human happiness and misery: we all live within society and—except for the few who are completely isolated—with friends and family. While most of the important research so far has been done in the workplace, the findings may apply to other situations as well.

At the top of your game

Most of us dread intense demands in the workplace, but sometimes such demands can lead to

a sense of control and even exhilaration. Basketball star Bill Russell once described the pressures of a pro game as follows:

"It usually began when three or four of the ten guys on the floor would heat up. . . . The feeling would spread to other guys, and we'd levitate. . . . The game would be in the white heat of competition, and yet somehow I wouldn't feel competitive . . . I'd be putting out the maximum effort . . . and yet I never felt the pain. My premonitions would be consistently correct. . . . There have been many times in my career when I felt moved or joyful, but these were moments when I had chills pulsing up and down my spine."

Few of us can rack up wins for the Boston Celtics. Yet many occupations (including some that are unpaid, such as raising children, doing community work, or playing an instrument for pleasure) can, under the right circumstances, provide great challenges and intense satisfactions—that same sense of cohesion, accomplishment, and control that Russell describes. A sense of personal control may, in fact, be a critical factor in maintaining health. The evidence is strong and growing that *people whose lives or jobs make high demands on them but allow little latitude for decision-making have higher rates of many diseases.* Indeed, the risk of illness for such people is two to four times what it is for others, independent of all other risk factors.

Though it's not known exactly how unsatisfying jobs and unhappy lives might make people sick, it's likely that they interfere with some general integrating system of the body—the nervous, hormonal, or immune system. The evidence is also strong that social support—that is, involvement with family, friends, and community—can buffer the impact of such social stress.

Low levels = high strain

Healthy Work, . . . published by Basic Books, offers an excellent summary of recent research in this field. Its authors, Robert Karasek of the University of Southern California and Dr. Töres

Theorell of Sweden's National Institute for Psychosocial Factors and Health, divide occupations into four categories:

Active jobs: heavy pressure to perform, but leeway allowed for problem-solving. Examples are doctors, engineers, farmers, executives, and other professionals. Hours may be long, but are partly at the worker's discretion. There are chances to advance and learn new skills. Initiative is part of the job description.

Low-strain jobs: self-paced occupations. Examples are tenured professors, carpenters, repairmen, successful artists, or any occupation with low demands and high decision latitude. (This idyllic category seems somewhat underpopulated in the authors' charts, no doubt because few such jobs exist in an industrial society. Furthermore, professors, carpenters, artists, and others can certainly experience high strain.)

Passive jobs: low demands on skills and mental processes, little leeway for learning or decision-making. Examples are billing clerks, nightwatchmen, janitors, dispatchers, and keypunchers. These jobs offer almost no latitude for innovation; sometimes workers' skills actually atrophy.

High-strain jobs: heavy pressure to perform but little leeway in decision-making. Examples are assembly-line workers, waiters, waitresses, nurses' aides, telephone operators, and any job where hours and procedures are rigid, where the threat of layoff may loom, where no new skills are learned, and where it may be difficult to take a break or time off for personal needs.

How stress makes people ill

Studies in the U.S. and Europe have consistently shown that people in high-strain jobs (which tend to exist mostly at the bottom of the job ladder) have the highest rate of heart attacks, while those in active jobs have the lowest rate. Passive jobs and low-strain jobs are in between. Research shows that those in high-strain jobs are also most likely to exhibit psychological disorders (including depression and exhaustion) and to take medications for depression; those at the top of the job ladder are best off by far in this regard.

Karasek and Theorell find, in short, that though "executive stress" exists, "it's the bossed, not the bosses, who experience the most stress" on the job. It's true, they point out, that the same problems (high demand, low decision latitude) can certainly affect executives.

Still, stereotypical "high-stress" jobs such as managers, electrical engineers, and architects have proven not to be associated with health risks, because professionals get to make more of their own decisions and thus feel more in control. Even when such risk factors as age, race, education, and smoking are added into the equation, those in the bottom 10% of the job ladder turn out to be in the top 10% for illness. Researchers have found that these workers have a four to five times greater risk of heart attack than those at the top 10% of the ladder, whose jobs give them a high sense of control.

A [study recently] published in the *Journal of the American Medical Association* and not covered in *Healthy Work* may in fact begin to explain the link between job strain and heart disease. A group of 215 healthy American men (age 30 to 60) in high-strain jobs were shown to be at least three times more likely to have high blood pressure than men without job strain and were also subject to actual thickening of the heart muscle. This is impressive evidence that psychological factors do play a role in physical disease.

Note on gender

Most of the research that Karasek and Theorell report was done on men—if for no other reason than that there are still few occupations with nearly equal proportions of both sexes. Nevertheless, they say, "women's average level of decision latitude is markedly lower than men's." Women fill more than their share of high-strain jobs, less than their share of active ones. Many of the high-strain occupations for women are newly created clerical jobs (for instance, computer operators in highly automated offices). This might have some impact on women's future health.

A little help from your friends

Social support on the job can mean many things: a comradely atmosphere among co-workers and between workers and management, a boss who treats his staff with respect, and the feeling of making a creditable contribution in a team effort. Labor unions and other kinds of employee organizations also provide social support. Indeed, depending on the circumstances, some high-strain jobs (for example, in restaurants, factories, and hospitals) can have some support built in—a good supervisor, regular breaks, or a sense that customers or patients appreciate the service rendered. According to Karasek and Theorell, support from co-workers and supervisors may be one of the most important factors in improving health and well-being in the work environment. Social support on the job acts as a palliative, mitigating the bad health effects of even high-strain jobs.

But what if a job is lonely? What if a person's colleagues are unhelpful or actively hostile? The authors of *Healthy Work* acknowledge the importance of social interactions with family and friends, as well as with the community, but did not evaluate these in their research. It's long been known (and we have often reported) that strong social ties can be a factor in maintaining health. However, a study of Swedish workers published in 1987 did suggest that in some circumstances "the psychosocial situation at work appears to have a greater impact on psychological well-being than do family situations."

Since high demand coupled with a low sense of control seems to create the most damaging strain in the workplace, it's reasonable to wonder whether the same principle would apply to family life and to many situations outside the workplace. . . .

Source: "Healthy Lives: A New View of Stress," *University of California Berkeley Wellness Letter,* June 1990, pp. 4–5.

FIGURE 3.2
Stress on the Job

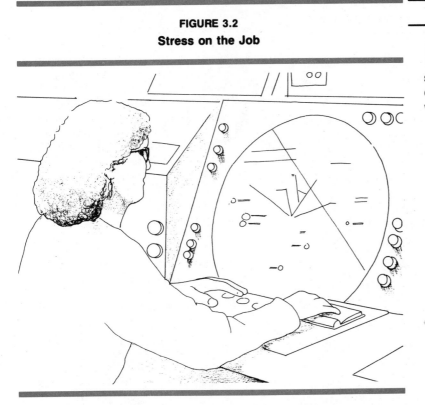

Air traffic controllers are under constant stress. The demanding nature of the work requires them to be alert, use careful judgment, and deliver peak performance at all times.

management technique provided by a stress-management program, some people will elect not to participate. Thus, whenever possible, a variety of techniques should be taught.

Informal Techniques to Modify Stress

Most people develop informal ways of coping with the problems of everyday life. Pursuing a hobby, taking a warm bath, watching television, reading for pleasure, listening to music, writing in a journal or diary, cooking, doing yard or garden work, and visiting with friends or relatives are all examples. These informal techniques are often highly personal. Some people, for example, are able to let go of their day's frustrations by weeding the garden. For others, this activity may produce more stress than it relieves.

FIGURE 3.3
Dealing with Stress Informally

Most people develop informal ways of dealing with stress. Many turn to a hobby that is of special interest, such as tending a garden.

Although informal activities do not replace a structured, well-planned stress-management approach, they can be used to supplement such a program. It is important, therefore, for people to discover which informal techniques work for them and then to incorporate these into daily life.

COUNTERPRODUCTIVE RESPONSES TO STRESS

Tranquilizers: Sedative drugs that have a calming effect, also known as minor tranquilizers.

Some frequently employed informal techniques for coping with stress are counterproductive and should be avoided at all cost. These include drinking alcohol, smoking, using **tranquilizers**, overeating, and resorting to violence. Although these behaviors may seem to relieve stress temporarily, in the long run they result in health problems and additional stress.

Many alcohol-abuse problems stem from stress. Many people consider having a drink at the end of the workday an acceptable way to unwind. However, the use of alcohol to relieve stress is a risky proposition that can lead not only to alcohol addiction but to many related and potentially tragic problems such as accidents caused by drunk driving.

People smoke for a variety of reasons. While many begin the habit because they want to appear more mature or because holding a cigarette gives them something to do with their hands, people also smoke to help control stress. Although nicotine is a **stimulant**, many smokers believe it helps them relieve anxiety and stress. It has also been shown to be an extremely **addictive drug**. Like alcohol use, smoking cigarettes can cause disease and even kill.

Nonsmokers under stress may use food in much the same way that smokers use cigarettes. In addition, former smokers often switch from smoking cigarettes to overeating as a stress-management device. Although eating food is certainly healthier than smoking, it, too, carries certain risks. Overeating or eating the wrong types of food can lead to obesity, high cholesterol levels, and tooth decay. Undoubtedly, there are healthier ways to manage stress.

Another potentially dangerous response to stress involves the use of tranquilizers. These drugs, available only by prescription, are typically used to treat anxiety or stress-induced sleep disorders. Despite the fact that tranquilizers are addictive, nearly 2.5 million adults take them regularly for extended periods of time. Seventy-five percent of these users are women. A total of 68 million prescriptions for tranquilizers were written in 1985. While this number is high, it is down from the peak year of 1975, when 88 million prescriptions were filled. [2] The important thing to remember about tranquilizers is that they are not substitutes for coping skills. They simply mask the symptoms of stress for a period of time. Although they may be useful temporary treatments for those undergoing severe stress, long-term use of tranquilizers has no place in a comprehensive approach to stress control.

Domestic violence, such as child abuse, spouse abuse, and elderly abuse, is a complex problem with many causes. Studies have shown, however, that stress is often a major contributing factor. The purpose of the stress response is to prepare the body

(continued on p. 62)

Did You Know That . . .

Eating as little as 1 or 2 ounces of carbohydrates can help the body produce serotonin, which calms the nerves. Low-fat selections will avoid putting on extra weight.

Stimulant: A chemical compound that elevates mood, induces euphoria, increases alertness, reduces fatigue, and, in high doses, produces irritability, anxiety, and a pattern of psychotic behavior. Stimulants include amphetamines, nicotine, caffeine, and cocaine.

Addictive drug: A substance that is physically habit-forming; stopping the use of an addictive drug results in withdrawal symptoms.

Tranquilizers: A User's Guide

"So, what can I do for you?" asked Dr. Smith (not his true name).

"I've been under a lot of stress lately," replied Patricia, "and I'm having trouble sleeping, so I'm tired all the time and I can't seem to concentrate at work. It's really getting to me."

Thousands of times each day, in doctors' offices across the country, patients recount similar tales of emotional distress. And like this one, with a young working woman seeing an internist, a great many of these office visits proceed along the following lines, with the doctor performing a routine physical exam and asking the patient a few relevant questions:

"Have you ever had trouble sleeping before?"

"No," said Patricia.

"What about your general health—any complaints of late?"

"None that I've noticed."

"Roll up your sleeve, please, so I can take your blood pressure. Do you get regular exercise?"

"Yes, I go to the gym and I jog."

"Ninety over 60. Very good. . . . How much coffee do you drink a day?"

"Two cups in the morning, and I don't drink it after noon."

"What about your alcohol consumption?"

"A couple of beers or a glass of wine when I get together with friends."

"Good. Is everything fine at home? Are you getting along with your partner?"

"Everything's great. It's just at work that I'm feeling things aren't going well right now."

"OK. You're having an acute sleep crisis, and I think that if we can give you a few good nights of sleep you'll be able to handle the situation at work better since daytime anxiety is a side effect of insomnia. Now I'm going to give you a prescription for Dalmane. It's a mild sleeping pill. Take it at bedtime for a few nights and you'll be back on track. If that doesn't work, call me and we'll move on from there."

"Thank you, doctor."

Up to the point when Smith put pen to prescription pad, his actions were thorough and responsible. Drugs like Dalmane are meant to be used short term to break a cycle of sleeplessness. During the 25 minutes he spent with Patricia, he searched for obvious causes for her insomnia. When none was apparent, he came up with an appropriate and reasonable action, namely prescribing sleeping pills for a few nights. It is not the approach all doctors would take, but it is well within the bounds of good medical practice.

The problem is addiction

The problem is that Patricia left the doctor's office with a prescription for 15 capsules of Dalmane—and three refills. Sixty pills total, enough to take one Dalmane a night for two months. More than enough for a few nights of good sleep. Enough, possibly, to give Patricia a problem far more severe than acute insomnia—sleeping-pill addiction.

It has been nearly 20 years since researchers first sounded the alarm that the family of drugs to which Dalmane belongs is addictive. The family, called benzodiazepines, includes the somewhat notorious tranquilizer Valium and at least a dozen other drugs. Each of them acts in complex ways as muscle relaxer, sedative, anti-anxiety agent and anticonvulsant. Depending on the person and circumstances, some of the drugs in the family are better at bringing sleep and others at bringing daytime calm. But each is potentially addictive, that is, can create a physical and psychological dependence.

Nevertheless, in the United States alone as many as two and a half million adults—over 75 percent of them women—have been taking these drugs on a regular basis for more than a year. And while there are some medical conditions, such as panic attacks and certain phobias, that do require extended use of these drugs, most prescriptions for benzodiazepines are meant to fight insomnia and anxiety.

Research has shown repeatedly that Dalmane and some of its chemical relatives are not effective at overcoming insomnia when taken for longer than a month or two. In fact, using Dalmane for longer than a month can induce insomnia. Other benzodiazepines are effective at relieving anxiety and panic for much longer periods, but the price is a dependence that shows itself especially clearly when the pills are withdrawn. Predictable withdrawal symptoms include tremors, sweating and anxiety. In the most severe cases withdrawal can bring on convulsions and psychosis, says Dr. Sidney M. Wolfe, director of the Public Citizen Health Research Group in Washington, D.C.

Some doctors hand out too many drugs

"Obviously, there are some physicians who ignore the data on these drugs and overprescribe," says Bonnie B. Wilford, director of the American Medical Association's (AMA) department of substance abuse. "But we have come a long way in educating physicians about the potential for addiction, and overall most doctors are more cautious than they were even 10 years ago about prescribing them in the first place, and continuing to prescribe them for long periods."

I set out, with the help of researcher Patricia Larkin, to see just how much physician attitudes toward these drugs had changed. We invented the story that Patricia told Smith and recounted it several times to various general practitioners, family physicians and internists in an urban area. We got the physicians' names from the Yellow Pages and from medical societies' referral services. I asked Patricia to help me with this informal sample, because health statistics suggest that doctors treat men and women with "mental health" complaints differently. We wanted to see if this assumption was true of the doctors in our small sampling.

One of the doctors I visited must have learned the AMA's lesson well. Not only did he give me a thorough medical exam—including a complete blood workup—but he also did not give me any pills to help me sleep or reduce the stress I described. After hearing my story, Dr. Rosen (not his true name) suggested I try drinking warm milk and taking 1,000 mg. of L-tryptophan an hour before bedtime. The brain converts L-tryptophan, an amino acid prevalent in milk, into serotonin, a compound thought to be one of the brain's own sleep-inducing substances. He also recommended that twice a day I put aside my work, turn on some music and just sit and relax.

"If that doesn't work," he said, "I might consider giving you a prescription for a few Xanax, a drug that's like Valium, and perhaps referring you to a psychiatrist to see if we can't figure out why you're having these problems."

While there are many more Rosens today than there were 20 years ago, some doctors are still unaware that Xanax, Halcion and other new-generation tranquilizers and sleeping pills are just as addictive as the Valium and Librium that have been around for at least 25 years. "It's those doctors we will continue to try to reach," says Wilford. "We have to get them to stop overprescribing, and we have to make them aware that some of their patients may have become dependent."

How they work on the brain

Introduced in 1960, Librium was the first benzodiazepine to meet the public. Hoffmann-La Roche brought out Valium in 1963 and it met with fast success. And although [the] addiction potential of benzodiazepines was recognized by the late 1960s, the pills were still considered much safer than the tranquilizers that preceded them. Over the years other agents from the same drug family were introduced to fight anxiety—Serax, Centrax, Tranxene, Clonopin, Ativan, Xanax and Paxipam. And Dalmane, Restoril and Halcion were introduced as sleeping pills.

"Benzodiazepines are more alike than they are different," says Dr. Andrew Mebane, head of the drug-abuse treatment program at the Ochsner Clinic in New Orleans. And the degree to which they produce their effects can, in part, be determined by a person's needs and chemistry. "Valium can make some people very agitated," says Dr. R. Michael Sanders, a psychiatrist at George Washington University Medical Center in Washington, D.C. So it is imperative that doctors know drug characteristics and their patients in order to match them properly. When this is done, benzodiazepines produce their tranquilizing effects by interacting with a group of brain cells in a tiny area called the locus ceruleus that controls the level of anxiety we feel in response to the various stresses encountered throughout our lives. They work in three stages: The drugs enter the brain and bind with benzodiazepine receptors. There they magnify the function of a brain neurotransmitter called GABA (gamma-aminobutyric acid). GABA inhibits the firing of anxiety messages from nerve cell to nerve cell.

"The holy water of psychiatry"

"These drugs have been immensely successful because they can effectively and safely treat one of the most prevalent health problems in the Western world: too much anxiety to function fully during the day and sleep well at night," says Godfrey Grant, a spokesman for The Upjohn Company, which makes Halcion and Xanax, the number-one selling brand of sleeping pill and tranquilizer, respectively. In fact, for short-term use, a month or less, these drugs are among the most effective and trouble-free that a physician can prescribe for any reason. One psychiatrist calls them "the holy water of psychiatry."

In contrast, earlier tranquilizers and sleeping pills, such as barbiturates, have been thought to interact with large portions of the brain. Side effects, including deaths from overdoses, were not uncommon. It is very difficult to overdose on Valium, Xanax or any other benzodiazepine, though combining it with alcohol can be lethal.

The presumed safety of these drugs has made them among the most popular drugs in the pharmacopeia, accounting for 7 percent of all prescriptions sold in the United States. Xanax, on the market since 1981, ranks sixth in terms of drug dollars in the United States, with doctors writing nearly 17 million prescriptions. While Valium is no longer the top-seller it once was, that merely reflects two things: It has far more competition in the marketplace, and its patent ran out in 1985, allowing sales of its generic. Physicians wrote more than 23 million prescriptions [in 1987] for diazepam, the generic form of Valium.

All told, Americans filled more than 68 million prescriptions for benzodiazepine tranquilizers in 1985. (Since no doctor can issue a year's worth of pills at one time, a person might be getting eight or 12 prescriptions in one year, as need continues.) This is down from the peak year of 1975, when an astounding 88 million prescriptions were filled. The numbers, however, have climbed steadily during the past three years.

Benzodiazepine sleeping pills are also very popular. In 1985, the last year for which figures are available, more than 20 million prescriptions for Halcion, Dalmane and Restoril were filled. Drug industry analysts estimate that figure is rising.

Though the number of prescriptions seems high indeed, some physicians believe that even more people need tranquilizers and sleeping pills. A study published by the National Institutes of Mental Health in 1984 found that 8.3 percent of adult Americans had suffered from an anxiety or sleep disorder during the six months preceding the survey. Only 23 percent of these people, however, received any kind of therapy at all. "I would argue that instead of these drugs being overused in this country, perhaps they are underused," says Dr. Mitchell B. Balter, a pharmacol epidemiologist and professor of mental hygiene at The Johns Hopkins University School of Hygiene and Public Health in Baltimore.

The pain of rebounding

Despite their legitimate applications and use, the problem remains that too often, patients continue using these drugs long beyond what the medical evidence would deem prudent. Some do so because their doctors prescribe too many pills. Smith's actions, for example, are not that unusual. Like many of his colleagues, he had good intentions, but he ended up overprescribing a potentially addictive drug. While not a common problem according to the AMA's Wilford, it happened 50 percent of the time in our sample.

In other instances, people seek out these drugs. They go to their doctors regularly, claiming their symptoms still exist, and ask for more. Sometimes, the doctor acquiesces. A study commissioned by the National Institute of Drug Abuse found, for example, that 69 percent of all benzodiazepine prescriptions written in 1986 went to men and women who had previously received a prescription for the same drug from the same doctor.

It is easy to see how a dependence develops. "A person will take Xanax for a month or so, then the prescription runs out and she goes through what we call rebound anxiety," explains Sanders. Though the mechanisms of rebound anxiety are not fully understood, researchers believe it occurs when nerve cells are no longer protected by benzodiazepines. The cells adapt to the drugs and become hypersensitive to anxiety. When the pills are removed, this suddenly becomes obvious.

Whatever the biochemical cause, rebound anxiety often can be worse than the initial anxiety. Sanders says it is very difficult to tell the difference between the original symptoms and the rebound symptoms. "A smart physician will realize what is happening and will help the person gradually wean herself from these drugs," he says. "But too often, these patients merely get another refill, so the problem continues."

Making it easy

Then there are those who don't heed the addiction warning signs and go from doctor to doctor just to get pills. I visited one doctor who seemed to be an easy mark for prescriptions. After I filled out a new-patient information form, Dr. Jones (not his true name) waved me into his office.

"What's wrong?" asked Jones.

"I've been under a lot of stress lately," I replied, "and I'm having trouble sleeping, so . . ."

"Wait here," Jones said, cutting me off in midsentence as he left the room. He returned a few minutes later with a 10-pack of double-strength Halcions. "Take a half-pill every night before bed. If these don't work, come back and I'll give you something stronger."

That was it. Five minutes, 20 doses of Halcion. He didn't even ask if I was drinking too much alcohol or coffee, both major causes of anxiety and insomnia. Fifteen years ago, Jones's behavior would have been nothing out of the ordinary. Today, thanks in large part to public pressure, educational efforts by professional societies and drug-tracking monitoring programs instituted by the AMA in conjunction with state governments,

few physicians hand out benzodiazepines so readily. According to Wilford, doctors now spend much longer with a patient before prescribing drugs.

Still, some believe that time constraints are one of the major reasons that overprescribing of benzodiazepines still occurs. "A family physician, general practitioner or internist sees maybe 40 people a day," says Sanders, "so there isn't always the time to take a thorough case history. Yet the patient wants relief. He or she wants to leave that office with something that will solve the problem. And the physician wants to help. Sometimes the doctor just helps a little too much."

Aside from Jones, the physicians that Patricia and I visited spent at least 20 minutes asking us questions and giving us routine physical exams in response to our complaints of insomnia and work-related anxiety. And except for Rosen, each doctor ended up giving us either a prescription or drug samples provided by a pharmaceutical company. The major difference between the responses that Patricia and I got was that her prescriptions were for more pills—and more refills—than mine.

Why women get more pills

"I'm not surprised," remarked Mebane of the Ochsner Clinic, when I told him of our informal survey. "Women are twice as likely as men to receive a prescription for benzodiazepines and are three times as likely to abuse them.

"It's not that women are more susceptible to drug addiction, it's because women are better health consumers: They are more likely to go to a doctor with complaints of anxiety or sleeplessness than men, so they often are prescribed these drugs. Men are far more likely to go get drunk."

In the bad old days of tranquilizers, drug companies used to run ads in major medical journals suggesting that Valium, Librium and the like were the perfect solution to a woman's problems. "Calm her immediately. Injectable Valium," read one ad. "You can't set her free. But you can help her feel less anxious," claimed an ad for Serax showing a nervous-looking housewife trapped behind a collection of mops and brooms resembling a jail cell. Just as bad was an ad for Librium showing a young woman, worried about going off to college. "A Whole New World . . . of Anxiety."

Today, drug companies are more subtle in their approach to doctors. "We are well aware of the abuse potential with these drugs and we spend a lot of time providing information to the physician about these problems," says Upjohn's Grant. "These drugs are very safe when used correctly and responsibly, and that's the message we want to get out to the doctors."

The mixed signals

Not everyone agrees that the message is without mixed signals, and often the message is mixed because the news is mixed. On the one hand doctors have seen journals this fall that report Xanax offers 92 percent relief in panic attack. In a 1,700-patient trial, a lot of people were protected from their own terror. In the same month, doctors may have heard that the University of Pennsylvania just began a major study—funded by the National Institutes of Mental Health—to discover how to treat patients who are dependent on therapeutic doses of benzodiazepines.

The main problem centers on the mistaken idea physicians have that the new-generation drugs are somehow safer, says Wolfe of the Public Citizen Health Research Group. "These drugs are as dangerous as older drugs like Valium and Librium because they produce faster rebound anxiety, which makes it more likely that patients are going to keep taking these pills long after they should stop."

Still, critics such as Wolfe concede, benzodiazepines are valuable for a great many people. "I'm certainly not advocating getting rid of them," he says. "We just have to be more honest about addiction."

—Joseph Alper

Source: *Health*, November 1988, pp. 35–39, 86–87.

---

for fight or flight. A person whose stress response has been triggered is prepared to release built-up tensions in a physical way, and may, inappropriately and dangerously, abuse those around him or her.

All of the responses discussed here are obviously harmful to health and should be avoided. Other negative coping techniques are not as obvious. For instance, excessive participation in activities such as sports, watching television, or reading can be counterproductive when they take so much time that important tasks go undone. Just as with other health strategies, balance and moderation are key words in stress management.

CHARLATANS AND INEFFECTIVE PROGRAMS

Over the past several years, stress has become a very great concern to both the public and the medical profession. As a result of this awareness, a whole cadre of stress experts has emerged, seemingly overnight. Although some of these practitioners are

(continued on p. 65)

What, Me Worry?

I'm worried—and for good reason: My cholesterol is high and my cash supply's low, my rent could go up and my stocks could come down. I'm worried about radon and fluoride; my friends all have CDs and I still buy records. There's the ozone, the Beltway, and handguns and herpes. My house plants look sickly and my mother may visit, my gums are receding and my employment's uncertain.

Like all incessant worriers, I never have a moment of relief. A psychotherapist friend says I have to learn to relax, because a person can't both relax and worry. That may mean exercise or a Jacuzzi or deep-breathing techniques, anything to keep the nervous system from becoming needlessly aroused. If that doesn't work, the routine may also have to include psychotherapy and/or something like biofeedback.

I knew I needed something, but I decided that, before I lie down on someone's couch or let them hook me up to funny machines, I'd explore a few other options. I turned to the ads in journals like *East-West* and to New Age shops around the city. Here's what my quest for the best off-the-shelf anti-worrying devices turned up.

EXPERTS IN ALTERNATIVE worry-management techniques recommended that I first enjoy the wonders of the Great Pyramid. Right. If I could afford a vacation in Egypt, I wouldn't be uptight in the first place. But that wasn't what they meant. Smaller-scale metal skeletons of the pyramids not only facilitate relaxation, I was told, but can do such magical things as sharpen razor blades.

Pyramids are available in a variety of sizes, including a three-foot-high floor model that you sit inside while meditating with your pets, house plants, and vegetables. The pyramid is supposed to act as an antenna that focuses cosmic and magnetic energy, which, in turn, is said to rearrange molecular structure. This, pyramid advocates claim, can mean anything from enhanced energy and reduced anxiety in people to renewed plant growth and longer-lasting vegetables. I'm not that concerned about my canned corn or turtles, so I bought a smaller model—one you wear on your head.

I hung around my apartment for a few nights wearing this pyramid hat. According to a booklet I got, people who use pyramids often feel total inner peace, a lessening of tensions, even a high state of euphoria. All I felt was a little worried that my neighbors would see me with this erector set on my head.

I decided to focus instead on other parts of my body—starting with my feet. The first relaxation item I tried was a set of five wooden dowels that you roll back and forth on the floor with one foot. This is supposed to massage your foot and make you happy. Since work is a great source of stress, I brought the thing to the office and put it under my desk. Within an hour my foot felt less tense, but I also got my sock caught in the rollers and tore a hole in the toe.

Next I tried the Dazey Foot Relaxer, which sends a few gallons of hot, bubbling water cascading around your feet. This really soothed my tired feet, but if you tip the tank slightly—as I did—when you're carrying it back to the sink, you learn that the back of the thing isn't sealed, which gives you something new to worry about: How do you get Epsom salts out of an Oriental rug?

Finally I decided to go after the deluxe treatment—the $199 Acu Vibe Foot Massager. This device has 196 vibrating rubber nodes, each of which is supposed to feel like a penetrating thumb. I spent an hour in the Sharper Image store downtown taking in 2,800 RPMs of blissful massage. I felt pretty relaxed, but then I realized that the security guard was staring at me, and I started to worry that I might get thrown out of the place. I got up to leave, but my feet had fallen asleep and my ankles were so relaxed they were numb. When the circulation finally returned to my lower extremities, I fled the place.

IT WAS BECOMING obvious to me that you can't focus attention on just one part of your body; relaxation, I decided, needs to be an entire mind-body experience. I considered all my options: polarity therapy, universal life energy, holistic body-work, bio-light healing, aura balancing, core energetics, chakra balancing, color and harmony dynamics, Reichian body education, rolfing, centering, spinal touch therapy, bio-magnetic futon therapy, and bio-energy field analysis. Decisions, decisions.

I finally settled on videotapes. There are all sorts of tapes on the market that are supposed to mesmerize you and, in some cases, lead you on a path to self-discovery and meditative bliss. It's like *Kung Fu,* but without the commercials.

The first one I tried was a half-hour tape that's supposed to let you commune with dolphins. Watching a few dolphins swim around at Sea World was relaxing for about 45 seconds, but then I got bored because they didn't do tricks like Flipper used to do. Next I tried the video aquarium, 60 minutes of tropical fish swimming around in your TV; then I tried the video fireplace, which lets you sit and watch logs burning in your set for an hour. I watched tapes of country roads, ocean waves, meadows, and sunsets. None of these tapes took my mind off my worries, so I went to Erol's and rented *Rocky II.* It didn't calm me either, but I enjoyed watching Sylvester Stallone get pummeled.

THE MORE I THOUGHT about it, the more I suspected that my angst was being caused by my job. Luckily, I happened on a book called *Pendulum Power,* by Greg Nielsen and Joseph Polansky, which explains how a pendulum can be used to determine if you're in the right profession.

The book told the story of Bob D., a successful dentist who had everything—a lovely home, a nice wife, money, two cars—but still was unhappy. Dr. Bob had been using a pendulum to locate bad teeth in his patients—swinging it over their teeth until it pointed to a cavity. One day it occurred to him that he could use the mysterious tool to pinpoint his own problems. In Ouija-board fashion, Dr. Bob asked yes-or-no questions, and the pendulum pointed to the answers. Lo and behold, he discovered that he didn't want to be a

dentist, but actually wanted to be a singer appearing at amateur shows.

Buoyed by Dr. Bob's story, I turned to the pendulum to figure out whether I was in the right profession. I was excited about finally learning my life's intended work, but I wasn't prepared for the results. Six times in a row the pendulum indicated that I should become Marion Barry's press aide. I spent two days breathing into a paper bag to end my hyperventilating.

Still, I felt I was on the right track. Someone suggested that I try self-hypnosis, which sounded like exactly what the doctor had ordered.

I bought a little hypnotic crystal ball and a book that explained how to develop suggestions for the subconscious mind. I came up with a half-dozen or so—"Every day, in every way, I'm getting better and better"; "Look out world, there's no stopping me now"; "What, me worry?" and so on.

I thought I'd try it out on my way to work. I boarded the bus, as usual, in Glover Park at the beginning of the line. It was relatively empty, so I held the olive-size crystal ball between my thumb and forefinger and began my self-hypnosis routine. Pretty soon my eyelids grew heavy and I fell into what was probably a deep hypnotic trance. As the bus headed downtown and more people boarded, I repeated my suggestions over and over to myself. When I finally opened my eyes I realized people were looking at me, and I started to worry that instead of silently repeating my choruses of hypnotic hyperbole, I might have been saying them aloud. I was so embarrassed that for two weeks I walked half a mile to catch another bus.

I HAD JUST ABOUT RUN out of options; it was time to go for broke. I sent away for a pendant that, when worn around the neck, is supposed to give you peace of mind by harnessing the energy that flowed from the pyramids. I think they must have meant the TV show *The $100,000 Pyramid,* rather than the Great Pyramids of Egypt, because for three nights I had nightmares that game-show hosts were asking me foolish questions.

Then I ordered Lourdes Miracle Water, which

is hermetically sealed in a crystalline reliquary and rushed by air from the sacred Grotto Springs in France. I was a little concerned that the water might not be the real McCoy because the company selling it was based at a post-office box in Paramus, New Jersey. But my little coffer of water arrived with a certificate of authenticity, so I hung the thing around my neck.

According to the testimonials I had read, shortly after receiving their Lourdes water people got pay raises, book contracts, or insurance checks, while others won at bingo. Shortly after my Lourdes water arrived I got a jury-duty notice.

I decided to try crystals, which their proponents hold out as having all sorts of curative and mystical powers. I was skeptical but still desperate, so I bought a book called *Crystal Love*, which comes packaged with a rose-colored quartz crystal. For only $8.95, I was told, I was going to find new love, harmonize my emotions and rekindle passion.

I programmed my crystal as instructed—by holding it to my heart, then putting it under my pillow—and tried to visualize my ideal mate in my dreams. The next day I put the love crystal in my pocket and went to happy hour at Rumors. I saw a woman at the bar who resembled the woman in my dreams and asked if I could buy her a drink. She told me to drop dead. This was a better reaction than I usually get from women. Maybe crystals are the answer.

—*Alan Green*

Source: *The Washingtonian*, February 1989, pp. 134–135.

legitimate, many others are interested only in cashing in on what experts predict will become a $15-billion-a-year stress-management industry within the next 10 years. [3]

Many practitioners promote a single stress-control technique, such as **biofeedback**, **Transcendental Meditation**, **yoga**, **progressive relaxation**, or physical exercise. While all of these techniques have merit and have demonstrated success in stress control, by themselves they provide an approach that is neither comprehensive nor personalized.

In addition to those whose programs are one-dimensional, there are a host of **charlatans** pushing unproven and perhaps even fraudulent stress-management strategies. One cosmetic firm, for example, has introduced a "stress cream" and "stress eye gel." A vitamin manufacturer has promoted a one-day supply of stress vitamins that can be purchased and taken if one has had a particularly stressful day. These vitamins are often sold at strategic places, such as airport gift shops, where a harried traveler is likely to feel a need to manage stress. The owner of a tanning salon recently took out a classified advertisement in a newspaper promoting the stress-reducing properties of his tanning booth. Persons, programs, and products such as these should be avoided.

(continued on p. 67)

Biofeedback: A method of learning to control involuntary bodily functions by mechanically monitoring one's own muscle tension, skin temperature, and brain waves, distinguishing between negative and positive responses, and trying to elicit more of the positive response.

Transcendental Meditation: A form of meditation that focuses on clearing one's mind by repeating a mantra.

Yoga: A system of exercises originating with the Hindu religion that are designed to promote control of the body and mind.

Progressive relaxation: A technique designed to bring about total relaxation through tensing and then relaxing one body part at a time.

Charlatans: Impostors or quacks.

A Cure for Stress?

"Put one hand on top of your head, with your fingers toward your face," the instructor says. "Take your two middle fingers and hook them into your nostrils and pull them up. Now stick out your tongue." *Voilà*—you've just made a "bat face." A kindergarten class this isn't; rather, making bat faces is part of a stress-management seminar for the Seattle Employee Services and Recreation Assocation. Former hospice worker C. W. Metcalf, the instructor, gives more than 250 lectures a year on the value of humor in minimizing workplace stress. Organizations like IBM, Hewlett-Packard and the U.S. Air Force have signed on. The cost for an all-day workshop on "The Humor Option": $6,500.

A few years ago stress was labeled the disease of the 1980s. Today stress management is fast becoming [a] boom industry. . . . Hundreds of companies now provide their workers with stress-management programs—everything from counseling to exercise to juggling. And a host of entrepreneurs have sprung up who see stress as the road to success. Many employees say they've been helped by these programs—but few companies can prove that stress management is really paying off. In a recent survey of 1,700 companies by the U.S. Department of Health and Human Services, only 4.2 percent reported that stress management had reduced health-care costs. Says Dr. Paul J. Rosch, president of the American Stress Institute, a nonprofit group: "Companies are throwing away millions of dollars on programs that don't work."

Rising costs: It's an especially worrisome problem, since employee tension and burnout have increased sharply. A recent study of California corporations showed that stress-induced job-health-care costs [doubled during the 1980s]. Other studies report that the cost of stress, including factors like absenteeism and rising stress-related compensation claims, is now an estimated $150 billion annually. The trend toward corporate mergers and restructurings threatens more salary cutbacks and layoffs, adding to anxiety in the workplace.

With billions at stake, companies are scrambling to develop cost-effective formulas for stress management. Many large corporations, such as AT&T, include stress reduction as part of more comprehensive "wellness" programs. The Long Island Lighting Co., which faces public outrage over its costly Shoreham nuclear power plant, spends $200,000 a year for a biofeedback consultant. And Weeden & Co., a Wall Street trading firm, hired International Health Systems, a massage clinic, to give on-the-job "acupressure" to its staff.

Stress entrepreneurs, meanwhile, are raking in revenues. Theodore Barash, former marketing manager for Weight Watchers, founded Stresscare, a Long Island company that creates customized regimens—everything from meditation to "hostility management"—at a cost of $75 to $150 per person. Dr. Jack Bagshaw abandoned a lucrative Marin County medical practice to start up Physis, a firm that provides relaxation exercises and fitness programs, for fees of $400 to $1,200. His clients include corporations like Pacific Gas & Electric Co. and BankAmerica Corp.

The stress business has also lured some highly suspect practitioners. "It's a field rife with charlatans," warns Rosch. Medical directors say they've been bombarded by pitches from phony experts touting everything from stress-reducing Caribbean cruises (tax-deductible to corporations) to "trampoline therapy" to liven up the office. Companies that lack time or resources to investigate the programs fully are apt to fall for promises of instant results at low cost. But even more sophisticated businesses may be unable to afford a comprehensive program. Instead, they may simply hand out brochures or bring in occasional speakers. Wells Fargo Bank in San Francisco saves the cost of a trained stress counselor by giving employees workbooks with step-by-step instructions to be used in conjunction with a videotape.

Do any of these programs really work? Many corporations cite figures showing improved productivity and reduced absenteeism, but "there is no study that has demonstrated the cost-effectiveness of these programs," says Lawrence R. Murphy of the National Institute for Occupational Safety and Health. But companies, tantalized by the enormous potential savings, look hopefully on any signs of improvement. Control Data Corp., which runs a comprehensive employee-assistance program that emphasizes stress management, estimates that it reduced total health-care costs by $3 million in 1983. The corporation now markets the program to 118 outside companies.

Medical experts maintain that companies can design a good stress-management program by following some basic guidelines. They should do an initial "stress audit" to evaluate sources of tension in the workplace; they should also give employees a wide choice of programs. "Some people may like an aerobics class, but others may only be more stressed by it," Rosch says. An effective regimen should include follow-up evaluation and reinforcement.

Competitive advantage: Of course, tension is always present in the workplace, and some is even healthy. "Stress is needed for optimum performance," says Dr. Kenneth Pelletier of the University of California School of Medicine in San Francisco. Businesses that learn to use stress positively will gain a competitive advantage by stimulating creative thinking and enhancing job performance—but so far few companies have done so. And critics say even the best stress programs don't address the corporate sources of tension, such as working for an incompetent boss. "The majority of employee stress is not caused by personal factors," says Kim Cameron, associate professor of organizational behavior at the University of Michigan. "The major problem is relationships with managers, lack of communication, stuff that we know how to fix." Once corporations relieve those sources of stress, employees will be even more productive. The best stress management may be good management after all.

—Penelope Wang in New York with Karen Springen in Detroit, Tom Schmitz in San Francisco and Mary Bruno in Seattle

Source: *Newsweek*, 12 October 1987, pp. 64–65.

CORPORATE PROGRAMS

Corporate America is awakening to the stress revolution. A California study showed that job-related, stress-induced health-care costs on the job doubled over a recent 5-year period. Other studies estimate that the cost of stress in terms of absenteeism, compensation claims, and loss of productivity is now $150 billion annually. [4] In addition, according to the National Council on Compensation Insurance, stress-related ailments accounted for about 14 percent of occupational disease claims by the late 1980s as compared to less than 5 percent in 1980. [5]

As a result of such statistics, an increasing number of companies now offer stress-management programs to their employees. Unfortunately, many of these employers do not provide *comprehensive* stress-management programs. Instead, they tend to offer one-dimensional approaches, such as relaxation training.

Did You Know That . . .

Among baboons placed in highly stressful "work" situations, those who sought out friends and allies were less prone to disease than loners.

Others provide one-day workshops or sponsor a series of speakers during the lunch hour. Some companies have even hired consultants to teach such things as juggling or developing a sense of humor to their employees. [6] While these activities may be fun and perhaps offer temporary relief from stress, again, they are not realistic long-term stress-management strategies.

One difficulty with many corporate stress-management programs is their limited focus. Some corporate programs, for example, offer techniques designed to help employees alter their perceptions of stressors and modify their responses to them but omit any techniques that might help workers reduce or control stressors. Controlling stressors may mean altering the corporation and the way it operates, which can be a threatening prospect to management. By providing employees with the skills to manage stress, a corporation may hope to absolve itself of the responsibility for providing a less stressful work environment. However, a company that is really committed to reducing its employees' stress levels will offer a comprehensive program that includes 3 levels of intervention: programs to teach stress control to employees, crisis services for those employees experiencing critically high levels of stress, and, perhaps most important, programs to promote organizational change.

One of the most important things to remember about stress is that individuals have more control over it than they may think. We can learn how to manage our stressors; we can learn to alter our perceptions of stressors; and we can learn skills to manage a stress response when it does occur. **W**

Controlling Stressors

THE PREVIOUS chapter stated that stress management entails 3 actions: controlling stressors, altering perceptions of stressors, and managing the stress response once it occurs. This chapter will examine the first of these strategies. Also called **environmental engineering**, the process of controlling stressors involves, in the words of one study, "willfully taking command and modifying one's own life." [1]

It is important to remember that because some stress is beneficial, one's goal should not be to eliminate all stressors but to identify and change those elements that cause the most problems and that are within one's power to control. A good place to begin is by identifying some typical methods used to alter stressors.

DAILY ROUTINE

Having too many commitments is a primary cause of stress for many people. There will always be days when events get out of hand, but when most days seem to fall into this pattern, it is time to step back and examine one's daily routine.

A major part of planning a feasible daily routine is to avoid scheduling events that either overlap or are too close together. For example, a student who does not get out of work until 12:55 should not schedule a 1:00 class that meets on the far side of campus. This would force him or her to leave work early or arrive at class late, either of which could cause stress. It would make far better sense to schedule either the class or the work hours earlier

(continued on p. 72)

Environmental engineering: Willfully taking command and modifying the stressors in one's own life.

Strategies for Managing Stress

We all suffer from stress, at least occasionally. But for the most part, we shrug it off as a fact of life and consult a physician only when stress takes its toll: as ulcers, skin breakouts, stomach problems, backaches.

But now there's a new group of experts—including psychologists, psychiatrists and social workers—who specialize in helping people learn to handle stress *before* it leads to medical problems. (For anyone with a physical symptom—such as hives, palpitations, backaches—self-diagnosis of stress is not advisable. See your doctor to clear up physical problems, then consider the following advice from the stress-management experts to prevent future problems.)

These experts employ a variety of techniques to help people learn to relax. While programs vary, generally they boil down to four strategies: changing your environment, learning to relax, becoming aware of stress patterns and learning new coping skills.

Environmental engineering involves taking a clear look at your day-to-day schedule and seeing what can be changed to make it less stressful.

Most psychologists agree that women, particularly, have a strong perception that they must do it all. Environmental engineering helps women realize that there are always alternatives, short-cuts, ways to lighten an overloaded work, home or social schedule:

• **Learn to let go** There are some tasks that must be done and others that can be skipped . . . or at least abbreviated.

Says Susan Dermit, a doctoral candidate in psychology at the State University of New York at Stony Brook, "The working mother who frets that on top of everything she now has to make her daughter a costume for the school play, and it must be great, needs to ask herself, Does this really matter in the long run? Does giving it up make me less of a mother? If you stop to think, you'll realize it doesn't, so why not forget it, or

rent a costume or throw together a simple one? Clinical experience shows that once you make this kind of self-demand a matter of *choice,* you reduce stress."

• **Take stock of all your roles** Make a list of all the roles you fill—mother, wife, sister, schoolteacher, daughter, friend, volunteer—and then set priorities. Says Joseph Procaccini, Ph.D., Loyola College, Baltimore, co-author (with Mark Kiefaber) of *Parent Burnout* (Doubleday), "You can get an *A* in parenthood this week if you accept a *C* in friendship. An *A* on the job tomorrow may mean a *B* as a wife." It's okay to switch priorities occasionally.

• **Take a fresh look at what you think others expect of you** You may be tougher on yourself than you need to be, or than others are. Laura George, Ph.D., a New York City psychologist, describes a patient who was becoming frazzled from rushing home after work to prepare hot dinners for her husband. "One evening, she timidly engineered a change by ordering in a pizza," says George. "To her surprise, her husband said, 'Great idea! Why don't we do it more often?' "

• **Always set your own priorities** Don't let someone else set them for you. Be assertive enough to tell the hospital auxiliary or the PTA that you're sorry, but maybe you'll be able to help out next year.

Relaxation strategies are ways to learn how to let go of stress. And mastering this skill is considered the single most important step in managing tension. Stress-management experts teach specific techniques, such as progressive muscular relaxation (relaxing one group of muscles at a time), meditation or deep breathing. But there are also simple methods you can practice yourself:

• **Schedule daydreaming time** and activities involving the senses. Listen to soothing music, take a shower or turn to a hobby such as knitting—a great meditation form for some.

• **Get yourself a pet** A study at Uniformed Services University of the Health Sciences, Bethesda, Maryland, indicated that interacting with an animal can bring about a decrease in heart rate and blood pressure.

• **Set aside time every day** just for relaxation. According to the experts, it doesn't matter *how* you relax; what matters is that you set aside time daily (you can use your environmental engineering skills to make room in your busy schedule). Stress specialists usually recommend twenty minutes of relaxation exercises a day, done in a quiet, peaceful environment.

Self-monitoring aims to make you more aware of your automatic patterns of stress reactions so that you can learn to break them.

• **Keep a diary,** and write down the circumstances each time you begin to get tense. The act of writing in the diary is therapeutic in itself. "When you can't gloss over something, but have to stop to describe it, you interrupt the flow of negative thoughts," explains Dermit. "We have patients who come in after a few weeks and say, Since I've been writing things down, they don't seem to bother me so much!"

Study your diary entries for clues to what contributes to your stress. By keeping a notebook full of such clues as where you were, with whom, what triggered your discomfort, and what your physiological symptoms were when you were feeling stressed, you can play detective and solve your own stress problem. You'll soon be able to break your stress pattern by changing the factors that lead to stress.

Coping skills are specific activities and helpful hints for dealing with daily stress. Some of the most important ones:

• **Exercise** When you begin to feel stressed, try walking or jogging. Research by James Blumenthal, Ph.D., at Duke University Medical Center shows that aerobic exercise seems to lessen stress responses.

• **Sleep is nature's medicine** Make sure you

get enough. "Don't discuss difficulties around bedtime," says David Reed, M.D., a Danbury, Connecticut, psychiatrist. "If thoughts keep you awake, get up and write them down; tell yourself you'll handle them tomorrow."

• **Turn stress to your advantage** Instead of chafing on the bus or bank line, for example, make it an opportunity to read a book or magazine.

• **Try postponing worries** that come up during the day, then give them your full attention during a specially set-aside half hour. The result can be a decline in how much you worry, if not the end of your worries, according to psychologist Thomas Borkovec, Ph.D., at Pennsylvania State University.

• **Stop putting things off** Procrastination adds tension, but task-oriented thoughts and actions reduce it. If you've invited business associates for dinner, for instance, start to plan the meal immediately. Better still, get going on one of the tasks involved.

• **Ignore outside influences** Don't be a slave to social pressure and other artificial stress builders. You don't *have* to go out every Saturday night, for example, just because others do.

• **Reward yourself** when you successfully handle a stressful situation. Changing habits requires positive reinforcement.

• **Ask for help** It's no admission of failure to seek professional help if you feel overwhelmed. A trained eye can often see things you're blind to.

Finally, says Richard Friedman, Ph.D., of the State University of New York at Stony Brook, "Be patient and committed. Invariably, people who put time and effort into learning stress-management skills view it as one of the most positive aspects of their lives. It *is* possible to minimize stress."

RELAXATION

To cope with stress, add ten minutes of gentle stretches to our basic fitness routine. For most people, the neck, shoulders, lower back, hands and feet take the brunt of daily stress. Add the following stretches to your daily workout session (do 5 to 10 repetitions of each): • With head up, slowly turn head to the right, then to the left.

• Starting with head straight, slowly tilt right ear toward right shoulder, then left ear toward left shoulder. • With chin to chest, gently rotate head to right shoulder, then left. Keep neck relaxed. (Do *not* rotate head to the back.) • Circle shoulders to the front, then to the back. Follow with shoulder shrugs. • Shake out arms and hands as if they were wet and you were trying to shake the water off of them. Do the same with legs and feet.

• Get on all fours, and slowly contract your abdomen and round your back, then slowly release to starting position.

—Sylvie Reice

Source: *Ladies' Home Journal,* January 1988, pp. 46–47.

or later in the day. If this is not possible, the student should talk to both the employer and the instructor about making allowances for late arrival or early dismissal.

Planning ahead to avoid overcommitment is another aspect of managing one's daily routine. Students, for example, may need to plan their class schedules several terms in advance so that they do not have to take more than 1 or 2 difficult courses each term. Although extracurricular activities, such as clubs, intramural sports, or fraternities and sororities, can be important parts of a college education, too many of them may also lead to stress. A student who accepts a leadership role in a club should learn to delegate some of the work in order to avoid overload. Students are not the only ones who have trouble avoiding overload; many adults have the same difficulty.

LEARNING TO SAY "NO"

There are many reasons why people tend to overcommit themselves. In some situations, people think they can handle many activities only to discover later that they have, figuratively speaking, bitten off more than they can chew. These people should learn to estimate their own capacities realistically. Other individuals would really like to refrain from overinvolvement but find it too difficult to say no when asked to do something. Saying no in a polite but firm manner is a skill one can master with practice.

One useful strategy is to postpone your decision. Before you agree to a request, be sure you know how much time and commitment it entails. Postponing a decision until you have this information gives you time in which to think and, if the response is to be no, plan exactly how to refuse.

(continued on p. 77)

Why Are You a Bundle of Nerves?

SIGNS OF TROUBLE

Check off all symptoms that apply to you:

☐ Inability to slow down, relax or to occasionally do absolutely nothing

☐ Anxiety because things seem to be going wrong too often

☐ Unexplained loss of appetite, general lack of interest in food

☐ Racing or pounding heart

☐ Fear of being in open spaces, tendency to avoid such situations

☐ Inability to concentrate on one thing for any length of time

☐ Loss of sexual drive or pleasure

☐ Feeling of being trapped

☐ Frequent headaches

☐ Nervousness when left alone for even brief periods of time

☐ Fatigue, difficulty sleeping

☐ Cold hands or feet, aching neck and shoulder muscles

☐ Sudden, groundless fears

☐ Anxiety or tension lasting more than a few days

☐ Heart palpitations, shortness of breath

☐ Increased tendency to drop or break things, frequent minor accidents

☐ A sense of hopelessness about life, despair about the future

☐ Explosive anger in response to a minor irritation

☐ Diarrhea, nausea, vomiting

☐ Sudden tears, trembling

☐ Tendency to blame oneself whenever anything goes wrong

☐ Overeating, increased consumption of drugs or alcohol

☐ Frequent low-grade infections

☐ Menstrual distress

WORKING WOMEN VS. HOMEMAKERS:
Whose life has more stress?

Sandra, who is in her mid-thirties, works as a feature writer for the entertainment section of a local newspaper. Her job sometimes demands that she keep unusual hours. Her husband, Joe, a photographer, tries to arrange his schedule so he can help with housework and the care of the couple's two children, but Sandra still finds herself doing more than her share. If she has an interview that can be done only at night and Joe is not available to care for the children, it is Sandra who has to get on the phone to find a babysitter. Her search is not always successful. Once, with her three-year-old son in tow, she interviewed a rock star; when the little boy knocked over a lamp in mid-session, the star was not amused.

Both Joe and Sandra often feel that life is a constant juggling act. Sandra would like to entertain more, but getting the house ready for company seems too big a chore. She worries that she and Joe are getting too bogged down in work and family duties, and are losing touch with their friends. Sandra also tries to help out at her daughter's elementary school and feels guilty when she has to say no, which, because of her busy schedule, she often has to do.

Marjorie, a full-time mother and wife, is the same age as Sandra. She is married to a businessman who travels a great deal, so much of the day-to-day household managing is in her hands. The comfortable suburb in which she grew up and where she now lives has one major drawback—no public transportation. As a result, Marjorie spends a great deal of time chauffeuring her three school-age children to their various activities and driving her elderly mother to stores and doctors' appointments. Marjorie also does volunteer work at the town's nursing home two afternoons a week, serves as class mother for the fourth grade and is chairwoman of the Little League annual fund-raising social. Her husband, Rob, says she ought to cut down on her volunteer work, but Marjorie thinks that because she's not working she ought to do what she can for the school and community. She can rarely bring herself to say no when her help is requested.

Which of these women is more likely to be suffering from symptoms of stress? Most people would answer "Sandra." No question about it. After all, she has to juggle both a demanding job and her many family responsibilities. Why should Marjorie be stressed? She has it easy.

But of the two women, it is, in fact, Marjorie, the homemaker, who may be more susceptible to symptoms of stress. Stress, scientists tell us, is created when an individual feels oppressed by outside forces. When these forces are too great, people respond with a whole range of physical and psychological symptoms, from aching muscles to sudden emotional outbursts. And Marjorie is hardly immune to these forces. She is constantly "on call" for other people—her husband, her children, her mother—and the volunteer work she does is simply an extension of the same sort of caring for others that she does at home. Her job description, "mother," doesn't allow for vacations or quitting time. Sandra, on the other hand, has a perfect excuse for not doing something that might overtax her energies: her job. If Sandra starts to feel tired and grumpy, people will understand. She's working and raising a family, poor woman. How much sympathy would Marjorie get if she complained?

Recent research has uncovered some surprising new findings concerning women and stress. When Abigail Stewart, Ph.D., and Patricia Salt, Ph.D., two Boston University psychologists, studied life stress, depression and illness in 133 adult women, they found that, when faced with life changes, married career women with children reported feeling less depressed or ill than did homemakers. And in a major study of adult women that was funded by the National Science Foundation, Grace Baruch, Ph.D., and Rosalind Barnett, Ph.D., psychologists at the Wellesley Center for Research on Women, in Wellesley, Massachusetts, found that homemakers suffered more from strain, from a "pulled-apart feeling," than did working women.

IS IT BETTER TO BE BUSY?

To understand the role of stress in women's lives, we first need to realize that its causes are much more complex than we once thought. The old stress model, which might be called the "limited pool" theory, was a fairly simple one: Each person has only a fixed store of energy, so that every new role she takes on drains more energy from the pool. Naturally, a woman who is both a mother and a worker will feel more stressed than a mother at home, because she has to cope with more demands.

But a better model for understanding how energy and stress interrelate may be the "recharged batteries" model. According to this theory, when we are involved in an activity that excites and challenges us, we may in fact be increasing our energy store. We all know that if we come home exhausted after a hard day's work and just flop onto the couch and watch TV, we keep feeling tired. But if we get up and jog or play tennis or take part in some other sport we enjoy, we start feeling more alert and alive—and we can recharge our psychological batteries in much the same way. So it's not just how much a woman does that's important but also how she feels about what she does.

"I'm the type that likes to keep going," says Elise, a 40-year-old office manager and the mother of three children. "It bothers me less that I'm rushed than it would if I had too much time. I do have to manage my time, though, so I won't feel overwhelmed."

Elise enjoys her busy life, but she also keeps her schedule under control—another key factor in avoiding stress. One recent major research study, headed by Robert Karasek, Ph.D., associate professor of industrial and systems engineering at the University of Southern California in Los Angeles, found, in fact, that it isn't having a lot to do that can make a person sick—but having a lot to do with little say over how and when to do it. Psychological stress, Dr. Karasek explains, is best combatted by taking action. When people can't, when they feel powerless, both the nervous system and the cardiovascular system can be affected. Workers who had little control over their jobs were found, for example, to be four times more likely to develop heart disease than other workers—and heart disease has been tied to stress.

The researchers indexed a variety of occupations and found that a great many of the lethal "high-demand, low-control" jobs fell into the "female ghetto" category: sales clerk, waitress, cashier, telephone operator. The woman in the typing pool, in other words, runs a greater risk of suffering from a stress-related illness than the woman in the manager's suite. And while the studies were conducted on employed people, common sense dictates that control—or lack of it—is also an issue for homemakers.

"High-demand, low-control" aptly describes the lives of many women at home, whose days never seem to end. Says Emily, a suburban housewife, "My day is fairly frantic. There are a couple of hours when I do household things—folding laundry and such. I spend a tremendous amount of time chauffeuring the kids—driving them to Camp Fire Girls, swimming lessons—it's endless. I drop them off and do shopping errands. There are a million chores. I never get things finished. There's never a sense of completing anything."

Control is a very real issue for Emily. "I have felt very often that it would be much simpler to have a paid job, because a job is structured—I would know what to expect, and I could plan for contingencies. I remember one day when the furniture movers were here, trying to bring a couch into the living room, and the phone rang, and just then the baby threw up in the front hall. Women are expected to be such incredible jugglers. My husband doesn't understand this. He has a secretary at his elbow and he can just say, 'Mary, take this call.'"

HOMEMAKERS NEED RESPECT!

Emily knows that a lot of people don't appreciate what she does. In one ranking of occupations in order of prestige, homemaker was ranked *below* marine mammal handler, on a par with parking lot attendant. As a result, homemakers very often fall into the trap of not taking their own "work" seriously. They shrink from demanding time for themselves or asking for help with endless homemaking chores. But in the long run, this "selfless" behavior can cost them dearly.

A husband who helps with the child care and chores, on the other hand, can do much to alleviate his wife's stress—and not only by lessening her workload. Drs. Barnett and Baruch found that when a husband did help on a consistent basis, his wife's self-esteem was enhanced—the reason being that, by helping, the man was effectively telling his wife, "What you do is important enough for me to share in it." And self-esteem—feeling good about oneself—helps a person ward off the ill effects of stress.

Worker or homemaker, however, there is another kind of "selflessness" that a woman must watch out for. For the sake of argument, let us say that human behavior can be divided into two types. One is assertive, action-oriented and concentrates on the "I" rather than on the "we." This is called *agency* or agentic behavior. The other focuses on relationships—on caring and feeling for another or for the group rather than for the self. This is called *communion* or communal behavior. When we seek a promotion or plan a work project, we are acting in an agentic way. When we read to a child or let a friend cry on our shoulder, we are being communal. Too much or too little of either behavior can be dangerous to a woman's health.

In one study, Dr. Stewart of Boston University, assisted by Ph.D. candidate Janet Malley, found that the woman who constantly emphasizes the "we," who is always giving and feeling for others, risks stress and burnout. They cite, for example, the case of Annette, an elementary school teacher and divorced mother of two who spent all her time—both at work and at home—caring for very young children. When Stewart and Malley first interviewed Annette, she felt angry, pressured and out of control—a prime candidate for a stress-related illness. But a woman in such a situation can often take steps to ease the strain, and Annette did. By the time of a follow-up interview a year later, she had left the classroom for an administrative job that was less emotionally draining, and she was feeling much better. "I can see how people get burned out," she said. "I knew I couldn't take it forever."

Twenty-three-year-old Michelle, on the other hand—another of Stewart and Malley's subjects—had a more agentic orientation. The working mother of two toddlers—she and her husband were separated—she treated life as if it were a management problem to be solved. "She organized everybody else's time and arranged for their well-being," Stewart and Malley note in their study, "but she spent very little time in shared activity." She missed work fairly often due to illness and suffered from headaches—physical symptoms common to people who think they have to manage everything. The problem: Michelle had no time for *communion* in her life.

The women in the study who had achieved a better balance in their lives between agency and communion—between "I" and "we"—were found to be much better off in terms of overall health and well-being. Understanding the need for this balance can also help women to plan their activities. A homemaker, for example, might become involved in volunteer work that offers her action and decision-making opportunities as an antidote to the nurturing she does at home. A working woman, on the other hand, could determine whether she spends most of her time caring and helping (nurse, social worker, teacher) or organizing and directing (office manager, school principal, businesswoman), then make sure that her off-the-job activities provide a balance between that "I" and the "we."

CAN WORK KEEP YOU WELL?

New research indicates, however, that having a job—a good job that offers challenges, ego rewards and a source of self-esteem—can, in itself, be a buffer against stress. In the Wellesley study for adult women, for example, Drs. Baruch and Barnett found that women who scored highest in overall well-being were working wives and mothers in high-prestige jobs. One such woman, a school administrator, is quoted as saying, "It is quite nice to feel—how do I describe it?—a sense of personal accomplishment, the satisfaction of competing with women who are very good, or doing well. I find it stimulating."

These women had achieved a healthy balance between "I" and "we." However, they were *not* Superwomen.

Superwoman does it all. She zips home from work to bake cookies for the kids while whipping together a gourmet meal for her business associates who are due to arrive at 8 P.M. The women in the Wellesley study were just the opposite of the Superwoman. Their secret of stress avoidance lay in what they *didn't* do. Their jobs and incomes gave them the flexibility to hire help, to juggle their schedules in ways that were convenient for them and to dispense with chores that were not absolutely necessary.

Homemakers might be wise to follow their example. Where is it decreed that one's plates must shine, one's plumbing pipes must smell like roses and that ring-around-the-collar is a sin? Where did all this demand for perfection come from? From the American corporate establishment, says Harvard economist John Kenneth Galbraith.

Advertisers, says Dr. Galbraith, deliberately set out to equate love with the use of their products. A mother is depicted as demonstrating love for her children by putting fabric softener in her washload or by serving them something fresh from the oven—but at what psychological cost to homemakers? If having dishes that don't gleam or laundry that doesn't smell like pine trees means you're a slob, that's bad enough. But if it means you don't love your family, not being the perfect housekeeper can become a major source of stress.

What we must remember is that homemaking is a job, not a quest for sainthood. And like other workers, homemakers have a right to reasonable working hours, control over their work and relief from constant demands. A little enlightened self-interest may be the homemaker's best protection against the ill effects of stress. Too often, women at home have been reluctant to push for improved working conditions. But if they don't, in the long run it is not only they who will suffer, but their families as well.

—*Caryl Rivers*

Source: *Redbook*, March 1986, pp. 96–97, 187.

FIGURE 4.1
Too Much to Do

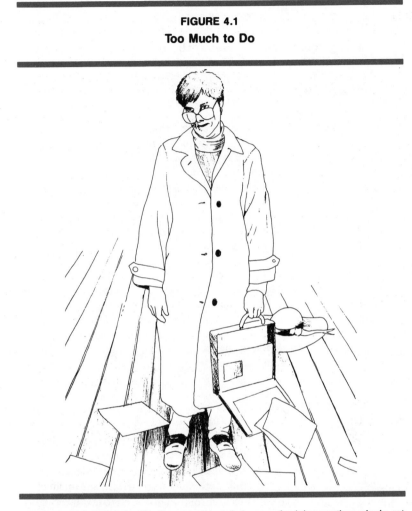

To help prevent a situation like the one pictured above, schedule your time wisely, set realistic goals, and learn to relax.

If you decide to refuse a request, you do not have to explain why. Everyone has the right to say no to requests without offering an explanation. However, if you think it is necessary to explain, be honest. Invented excuses are often weaker than the real reason and can make you feel guilty. Finally, whenever possible, try to provide alternative solutions. Suggest other people with similar skills or discuss ways the task can be completed without your involvement.

TIME MANAGEMENT

Time management means making the best use of the time you have available. Often the stress associated with overcommitment is not caused by a lack of time but by poor use of available time. Consider the following scenario:

> John has a math homework problem that he needs to solve. Immediately after class he returns to his room, reads the problem, and decides how he will approach it. He also decides, however, that he will wait to do it after supper. After supper, he again sits down, reads the problem, and reviews in his mind how he is going to approach it, but he also remembers he has a paper due tomorrow in health that he had better work on instead of the math problem. The next morning he sits down, reads the math problem, and once again organizes his thoughts. This time he hears the sound of ping-pong balls coming from down the hall and decides to see if he can get in a game or two. He has been working hard and deserves some relaxation. Thus far John has read and thought about his math problem 3 times and has yet to do any work on it. This is a perfect example of poor time management. John would have saved himself considerable time and stress had he set aside one specific time during which to sit down and complete the problem.

Time-Management Planning

Proper time management involves a variety of techniques. **Time blocking**, for example, entails setting aside specific blocks of time for specific purposes and then holding to that schedule just as rigidly as to a class or work schedule. The first step in this process is to identify each task that needs to be completed within a specific period of time. Next, information regarding each task should be gathered and the following questions asked:

1. *When does the task have to be completed?* Those tasks that have to be completed sooner should be placed first.

2. *Who should do the task?* Tasks that can be easily delegated to someone else can be removed from your list. If, however, it would take more time and energy to teach another person to do the task and supervise his or her work than it would take to do it yourself, the task should not be delegated. The exception to this is an ongoing or continuing task. Although it may take more time to teach the task this week, in future weeks time may be saved.

Time blocking: Setting aside specific periods of time for identified purposes.

3. *Where must the task be done?* Tasks that need to be carried out in the same location can be done at the same time. For example, Elizabeth notes that 2 of her tasks require library time. She decides to do one task Monday night and the other Tuesday night. Let's assume that it takes her 15 minutes to get to the library and 15 minutes to get back home. If she makes 2 trips to the library, she wastes at least a half hour. In addition, she may take additional time to find a desk, locate resources, and get settled.

4. *How much time will the task require?* Establishing the time each task will require can be difficult. In general, people tend to underestimate, which contributes greatly to overload problems. One solution is to plan a 15 to 20 percent cushion for new and unfamiliar tasks. For example, if you think it will take 60 minutes to read a chapter, plan for 70 minutes.

   Unexpected interruptions are another factor that can make our estimations of time inaccurate. These can include visitors or telephone calls, personal illness, and relationship problems. While some of these can be controlled, others are beyond our control and will force changes in our planned schedule. Persons who are flexible and can adapt to change handle these stressors much better than those who are rigid and become extremely anxious and frustrated when their schedules are disrupted.

5. *What priority does the task have in relation to the other tasks?* Prioritizing tasks is critical to time management. Tasks can be divided into 3 priority areas: those that are essential and must be done immediately; those that are essential but can be put off until a later time without harm; and those that are not essential but would be nice to accomplish.

Once all tasks are rated, start scheduling the activities on your calendar according to those that received the highest priority. If additional time exists after the highest priority tasks are included, schedule time for those tasks receiving lower priorities. But if there is not even enough room on the calendar to include all the highest priority items, you may have to reprioritize. If this is not possible, it is probably a good indication that you are in an overload situation.

The calendar in Figure 4.2 is an example of how one student, Leslie, uses time blocking over a one-week period. Leslie has placed on her calendar all the activities she will do throughout the week. Some of the activities are scheduled at a prescribed

(continued on p. 81)

FIGURE 4.2
Leslie's Calendar: Finding Time for Fitness

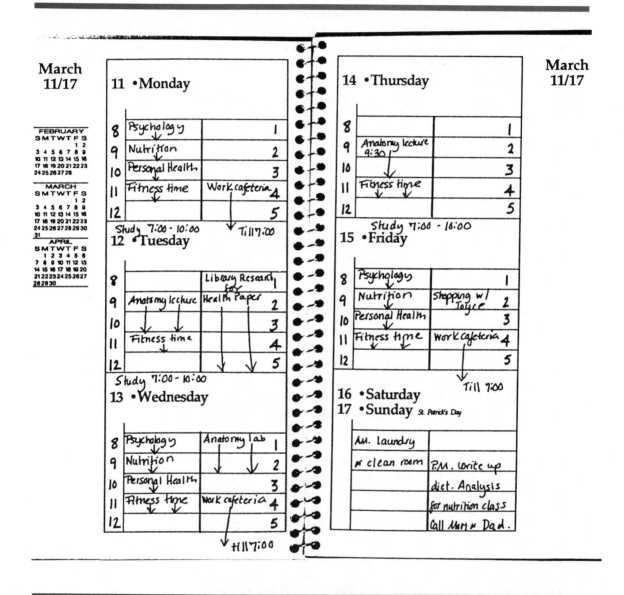

This calendar shows how Leslie, a busy college student, has used time blocking over a one-week period. She has scheduled in fixed activities such as classes and work but has also scheduled in her own fitness time daily, thus placing a high priority on her personal health.

time, and she has no flexibility in placing them in her calendar. Classes and work are examples. Leslie has also scheduled her own fitness time at 11:00 A.M. daily. By doing this, she is placing a high priority on her personal health.

After filling in all the required activities, Leslie notices several large blocks of time that are open. Monday, Tuesday, Thursday, and Friday afternoons are all fairly open. This week she has decided to spend Friday afternoon shopping with her friend Joyce and Tuesday afternoon doing research for a term paper that is not due until later in the term. By working on the research now, she may avoid the stress of having to rush later.

Sunday through Thursday evenings she sets aside the 3 hours from 7:00 P.M. to 10:00 P.M. for her routine class assignments. It is quite possible that some nights she may not need all 3 hours, while on other nights she may need more. Therefore, she allows for flexibility during this time period.

It is also important to notice that she has left significant blocks of time unscheduled. These periods are left free to accommodate unplanned events or for tasks that may take more time than expected. This kind of flexibility is critical to the success of any schedule.

Other Time-Management Skills

Other techniques that can be used to manage time include:

1. *Minimizing interruptions* is important if you are doing work that requires concentration. Shut the door to your room or office and do not answer the phone. Turn off the radio or television and, if necessary, shut the drapes. These tactics make it easier to focus attention on the task at hand.

2. *Controlling the mail* is another way to save time. When looking through the mail, respond immediately whenever possible. Throw junk mail away. Stack bills together and set aside a time to deal with them all at the same time. Whenever possible, have your name removed from unnecessary mailing lists.

3. *Manage the time you spend in meetings.* If you can, make a decision by yourself without calling a meeting. When a meeting must be called, set a specific time, develop an agenda, and stick to it. Keeping the meeting size small can help a group to stay focused on its task, reduce conflict, and increase efficiency.

FIGURE 4.3
Getting Organized

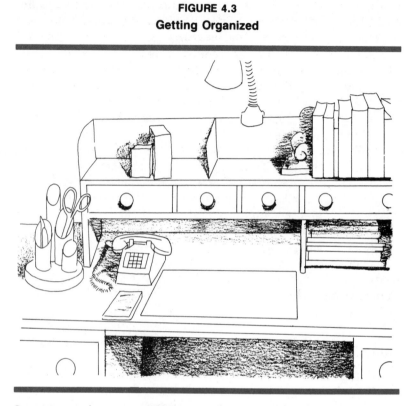

Organizing your desk is a good way to increase efficiency. Try sorting work into categories that make sense for you.

4. *Organizing your desk and files* is another way to increase efficiency and save time. Organize work into categories that make sense for you. For example, separate the papers that must be looked at today, those that must be dealt with this week, and others that can wait until next week. Another way to organize is to have a stack of papers that needs a written response, a second stack that requires a personal or telephone response, and a third stack that must be read but needs no response. Using tier trays, dividers, and file folders can make organizing everything a much easier task.

5. *Being aware of your own work preference* is an important aspect of time management. Morning people, for example, do

their best work early in the day, whereas others are slower to get started but work well later in the evening. It is usually best to do the most difficult tasks during the time of day when you work best. Use those periods of time when you are not at your best to do the more mundane, less creative, and less demanding tasks.

6. *Task segmentation,* or breaking large tasks into smaller ones, is another technique to help reduce stress. For example, writing a term paper can appear to be an enormous task when considered as a whole. But it can easily be divided into 6 smaller tasks: (1) deciding on the topic, (2) locating sources, (3) reading the sources, (4) outlining and organizing, (5) writing, and (6) final production and proofreading. Each of these smaller tasks seems more manageable and allows for personal satisfaction after completing each sixth of the paper rather than waiting until the entire paper is completed. In addition, it is easier to find blocks of time in which to work on a portion of the paper than to complete the project as a whole.

AVOIDANCE AND CONFRONTATION

There are certain people or situations that, for some reason, always seem to cause stress. For example, Sue's job is stressful because she works with a person who is always trying to tell her what to do. There are several techniques Sue can employ to manage this situation. She can attempt to maintain her present position but avoid all contact with the person. She can ask for a transfer to a different position that would not require her to interact with the bothersome person, or she can elect to change jobs. In each case, Sue is taking the responsibility to avoid the stressor.

It may, however, be wiser for Sue to confront her stressor than to avoid it. She may want to speak directly to the person causing the problem, or she may opt to take the matter to her supervisor for resolution. In either case, she has confronted the problem. If the situation still does not improve, Sue must then make the decision to live with the stressor, recognizing it as something she cannot control, or she can seek a new position in another department or organization. Because the decision is hers, she is in control.

(continued on p. 85)

Did You Know That . . .

A California study of male heart-attack victims showed that Type A personalities survived longer than gentler Type Bs.

Your boss berates you for a botched report. Do you: (a) lash out in anger; (b) hole up in your room and mourn; (c) quit on the spot and look for a new job; or (d) run up your phone bill pouring out the story? Researchers are discovering that your coping style—the way you react to stressful events in your life—is closely linked to your personality type and may indicate whether you'll fall prey to stress-related ailments.

Caution: Your Stress Style May Be Hazardous to Your Health

In a study of 406 people at the Gerontology Research Center in the National Institutes of Health, Robert R. McCrae, Ph.D., research psychologist, examined 27 coping mechanisms and their corresponding personality characteristics. He found that certain kinds of people will react predictably to stress. For example, people who frequently experience negative feelings (guilt, anger, sadness) tend to handle stress by venting their frustration on others or blaming themselves. Warm, gregarious people are more likely to cope rationally. Open-minded people are prone to be inquisitive and to use humor in response to stress, and people who resist change turn to faith—faith, perhaps, in their doctor, in the President or in things always turning out for the best.

Type A? You're Okay

So which of these personalities is most vulnerable to stress in the first place? Researchers now say you no longer need fear the hard-driven, competitive characteristics of the Type A personality, because they don't make you any more stressed than the most bovine Type B.

What *may* make you prone to stress are other dimensions of your personality, particularly your levels of hostility. According to Ted Dembroski, Ph.D., professor of psychology at the University of Maryland in Baltimore, people who are uncooperative and antagonistic are much more susceptible to heart disease at an early age than people who are agreeable and easygoing. Similarly, Redford Williams, M.D., professor of psychiatry at Duke University in Durham, North Carolina, discovered that individuals who exhibited a cynical mistrust of others, frequent expressions of anger, and aggressiveness were also the most stress-ridden.

Dr. McCrae's study confirmed that those most prone to stress are the least able to handle it. When his subjects rated coping styles in terms of their capacity to reduce stress, lashing out at others fell at the bottom of the list, along with self-blame, wishful thinking and indecisiveness. The [9] most effective methods: faith, seeking help, taking rational action, drawing strength from adversity, expressing your feelings, changing yourself to meet the situation, humor substitution, restraint and positive thinking.

What's central to most coping mechanisms is that they help you gain a sense of control over the situation. Remember, your coping style is not etched in stone, but can be learned and practiced. Experts suggest you try different tactics when dealing with difficult situations. "If escaping isn't working, try humor," says Dr. McCrae. "Take a cafeteria approach. That way you can eventually figure out what's best for you."

—Diane Fields

Source: *Mademoiselle*, April 1989, p. 158.

NUTRITIONAL MANAGEMENT

Nutritional problems can be stressors in themselves or may increase the effects of other stressors. Although much research remains to be done in this area, the information now available can be important in a comprehensive approach to stress management. There is both a direct and an indirect link between nutrition and stress. Scientists have found that the physical stress of illness and injury can lead to a greater need for proteins, vitamins, and minerals. These increased requirements do not diminish until the body has repaired itself completely. Although there is no conclusive evidence that emotional stress directly increases one's nutritional requirements, this type of stress can affect eating behavior. Some people respond by eating more, others by eating less. Depending on the severity of the change, the results can range from nutritional deficiency to obesity. If the behavior continues for a long enough time, the individual's health can be adversely affected. [2]

Certain substances found in foods can create a stress-like response and may themselves be considered stressors. These substances, called **pseudostressors**, actually mimic sympathetic nervous system stimulation. The most common of these is caffeine, which is found in coffee, tea, chocolate, and many carbonated beverages. [3] (See Table 4.1 on page 86.)

Large amounts of caffeine can produce symptoms similar to those of a stress response. Caffeine can also exacerbate a stress response that is already occurring. Other frequently noted symptoms of excessive caffeine use—more than 250 milligrams per day—include anxiety, irritability, diarrhea, and inability to concentrate. In the United States, coffee is the most common source of caffeine, and the average 6-ounce cup of brewed coffee contains approximately 100 milligrams. Americans over the age of 14 consume, on the average, 3 cups of coffee per day.

Pseudostressors: Substances such as the caffeine in coffee, tea, chocolate, and cola beverages that actually mimic sympathetic nervous system stimulation.

Table 4.1 Estimated Amount of Caffeine in Selected Foods

Item	Amount	MG Caffeine
Instant coffee	5 oz	58–70
Percolated coffee	5 oz	90–125
Drip coffee	5 oz	125–155
Decaffeinated coffee	5 oz	2–5
Black tea (bag)		
1 min. brew	5 oz	28
3 min. brew	5 oz	44
5 min. brew	5 oz	55
Canned ice tea	12 oz	22–36
Cocoa beverage	6 oz	5–10
Chocolate drink	8 oz	8–20
Milk chocolate	1 oz	6
Baking chocolate	1 oz	35
Sweet chocolate	1 oz	20
Colas, including diet types	12 oz	32–65
Soft drinks (will be listed on the label)	12 oz	0–52

Source: *From Your Home Advisor,* University of California Cooperative Extension, Anaheim, CA, November 1981.

While moderate amounts of caffeine have no harmful effects on most people, excessive amounts (more than 250 milligrams per day) can contribute to stress. This table lists the estimated quantity of caffeine found in a variety of common beverages and foods.

B-complex vitamins: A group of 8 vitamins that primarily act as coenzymes, helping enzymes metabolize food.

Metabolize: To chemically alter substances in the body, by breaking them down to produce energy or building them up to consume energy.

Excessive levels of sugar in the diet may also contribute to stress in several ways. First, the metabolism of sugar in the body requires the use of **B-complex vitamins**. The typical refined sugars most Americans consume provide only energy and no B vitamins or other nutrients. Therefore, the body must use B vitamins provided by other foods to **metabolize** sugar. This may lead to B vitamin depletion and to problems controlling stress, since several of the B-complex vitamins are important components in the stress response. Deficiencies of the B vitamins thiamine, pantothenic acid, and pyridoxine can lead to anxiety, depression, insomnia, and cardiovascular weakness, while riboflavin and niacin deficiencies have been known to cause stomach irritations and muscle weakness. [4]

Hypoglycemia, or low blood sugar, is a condition that can stem from sugar intake. People under a lot of stress often pay little attention to diet and may eat too much sugar-laden food. When there is too much sugar present in the bloodstream (a condition called **hyperglycemia**), the body releases a large amount of **insulin** to metabolize the sugar and channel it through various bodily tissues. Unfortunately, during this process the blood can lose too much sugar, causing a hypoglycemic state. Symptoms of hypoglycemia include irritability, anxiety, fatigue, trembling, and increased cardiac activity. Note that these symptoms are very similar to those associated with a stress response, so a person already under stress who suffers a hypoglycemic reaction has a double problem. [5]

Although the B-complex vitamins are essential to the healthy management of stress, the nutrient most associated with the stress response is vitamin C. The **pituitary** and the **adrenal glands** contain the highest concentrations of vitamin C in the body, and both are highly involved in the stress response. However, the exact effect of stress on these vitamin stores is unknown.

In fact, although many vitamin advertisements espouse the benefits of nutritional supplements as a protection against stress, there is little, if any, scientific evidence to support such claims. Most doctors would agree that maintaining a well-balanced diet is a more effective health-protective strategy than relying on nutritional supplements. [6]

NOISE

Another way to reduce stress levels is to avoid exposure to noise. Noise can produce a stress response in 3 ways: (1) as a physiological reaction caused by stimulation of the sympathetic nervous system, (2) as a subjectively annoying and displeasing experience, and (3) as a disruption of ongoing activities.

In the first instance, a loud or sudden noise may immediately stimulate an alarm reaction and a stress response. An example of this is the wind causing a door to slam shut. In the second situation, a subjective interpretation of noise can produce a stress response. For some, loud rock music might be enjoyable; for others, it can be quite stressful. Finally, noise that disrupts ongoing activity can be stressful. For example, someone whispering or loudly chewing gum in a library while others are trying to concentrate is often disruptive, and this can trigger a stress response.

Did You Know That . . .

Experiments with rats show that when stress depletes the body's store of B vitamins, hair turns gray.

Hypoglycemia: An abnormally low level of sugar in the blood that is often associated with diabetes.

Hyperglycemia: An abnormally high level of sugar in the blood that is associated with diabetes.

Insulin: A protein produced by the pancreas that allows glucose to be taken up by a cell and used as fuel. A person without insulin or insensitive to insulin has diabetes.

Pituitary: A small, pea-sized gland located at the base of the brain that regulates and controls the activity of the other endocrine glands (glands, such as the thyroid and adrenal, that secrete hormones directly into the bloodstream).

Adrenal glands: A small, triangular-shaped pair of glands located on top of the kidneys that secrete hormones, including adrenaline (epinephrine), directly into the bloodstream.

SUMMARY

This chapter discusses a number of ways to control and modify stressors. If used properly, these techniques can reduce the frequency of the stress response. All of us have the ability to manipulate our environment to reduce or eliminate at least some stressors. Whether through time management, avoidance, confrontation, or nutritional management, many stressors can be controlled, modified, or eliminated. In the final analysis, controlling stressors is each individual's responsibility. It is something you have to do for yourself; no one else can do it for you. ▧

Altering Individual Perception

S AM IS A COLLEGE STUDENT who has many female friends and seldom has difficulty getting dates. Lately he has noticed an attractive woman in his health class. When he asks her out, she turns him down, explaining that she has too much studying to do, but she would enjoy a date with him some other time. Sam immediately perceives the refusal in a negative light. How could she turn him down? Doesn't she have all weekend to study? What if his friends find out? Not only do these initial thoughts create stress, but he continues to focus upon them, which causes further stress.

In this instance, the real source of stress is Sam's reaction. The event and its follow-up would have been much less stressful for Sam if he had viewed the woman's refusal not as a personal slight but instead as a demonstration of her commitment to her studies. This chapter will identify some of the ways in which perception can influence stress and examine some techniques you can use to alter stress-producing perceptions and personality traits.

STRESS-PRODUCING PERSONALITY TRAITS

There are several personality traits that can make situations and perceptions more stressful than they should be. Learning to overcome and avoid each of these traits is one of the most useful elements of any stress-management program.

Procrastination

Those who habitually put off doing tasks they know need to be done are engaging in **procrastination**. Procrastinators have enough time in which to do their work but choose to put it off

Procrastination: The practice of putting off a required task or action in the absence of a valid reason.

Did You Know That . . .

Studies show procrastinators are motivated by underlying fears—of authority, of being judged and rejected, and of missing out on life.

FIGURE 5.1
Procrastination

Procrastinators usually have enough time in which to do their work but choose to put it off until the last minute. These people experience stress because of the way they handle a situation.

until the very last minute. This is not a problem for those people who do their best work when faced with a deadline. For many others, however, last-minute pressure creates a debilitating anxiety that hinders productivity. In addition, these pressures may occur so frequently that their bodies never have the chance to recover.

People who suffer stress as a result of procrastination need to do more than just improve their time-management skills. To be sure, learning how to set priorities and establish realistic work schedules, as discussed in the previous chapter, can help relieve the stress associated with procrastination. In most cases, however, procrastination is not the real problem but a symptom of the problem. That is to say, procrastination often arises not so much

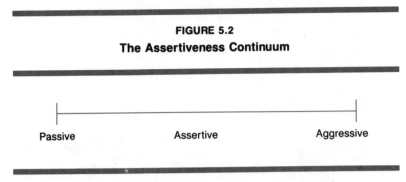

FIGURE 5.2
The Assertiveness Continuum

Passive   Assertive   Aggressive

When confronted with a problem, our response may be passive, assertive, or aggressive. An assertive response to a problem is the best way to avoid stress.

from the level of the demands on the procrastinator but from his or her perception of those demands. In such cases, it is the individual's perceptions that must be dealt with in order to relieve stress.

Lack of Assertiveness

Writing the monthly report for her department is not part of Janet's job description, but her boss has asked her to do it for him. Not wanting to displease him, she takes time out of her busy schedule to do it and thus fails to meet an important deadline for her own work. This is not the first time that Janet's lack of **assertiveness** has created stress in her life. She is a prime candidate for stress reduction through assertiveness training.

When confronted with a problem such as the one faced by Janet, our response may be passive, aggressive, or assertive. When people deal with a situation passively, they usually appear shy, quiet, and introverted. During interactions with others, their voices are often weak, hesitant, and wavering; their eyes avoid direct contact, and their hands fidget. They often end up being emotionally hurt by others because they do not stand up for their rights. Passivity in the face of problems often leads to a buildup of frustration, anger, and stress.

Aggressive behavior, on the other hand, is not a good approach either. People who respond aggressively appear obnoxious, abrasive, and insensitive. During interactions, their voices are often loud and demanding, and they appear angry and hostile. In their eagerness to get their own way, they often trample on the rights or feelings of others. Aggressive people can lose friends and damage relationships with colleagues, factors that contribute to a stressful life-style.

Assertiveness: The ability to declare and work on behalf of one's needs without alienating others or violating their equally valid needs.

FIGURE 5.3
Assertiveness

When responding assertively to a situation, it helps to use assertive body language. This includes making direct eye contact, confident posture, a firm voice, and appropriate facial expressions.

An assertive response is the best way to avoid stress. People who respond assertively are confident, friendly, and self-expressive about their needs, but not loud or abrasive. They are aware of their rights but can ask for them in a nonthreatening manner, without hurting others. Assertive responses lead to less stress and more satisfactory relationships.

The following 6-step process has helped many people develop more assertive behavior: [1]

1. *Learn to identify the 3 basic styles of interpersonal behavior* just discussed. Until people can identify their own aggressive and passive traits, little can be done to improve assertiveness.

1. Look at your rights, what you want, what you need, and your feelings about the situation. Let go of blame, the desire to hurt, and self-pity. Define your goal and keep it in mind when you negotiate for change.

2. Arrange a time and place to discuss your problem that is convenient for you and for the other person. This step may be excluded when dealing with spontaneous situations in which you choose to be assertive, such as when a person cuts ahead of you in line.

Developing the Working Plan: A Step-by-Step Approach

3. Define the problem situation as specifically as possible.

4. Describe your feelings using "I messages." An "I message" expresses your feelings without evaluating or blaming others. Rather than say, "You are inconsiderate" or "You hurt me," the message would be, "I feel hurt." "I messages" connect the feeling statement with specific behaviors of the other person. For example, "I felt hurt when you left without saying good-bye." Contrast the clarity of this message with the blame statement, "I felt hurt because you were inconsiderate."

5. Express your request in one or two easy-to-understand sentences. Be specific and firm!

6. Reinforce the possibility of getting what you want by stating the positive consequences should the other person cooperate with you. If necessary, state the negative consequences for failure to cooperate.

Source: M. Davis, E. R. Eshelman, M. McKay, "Assertiveness Training—Step Four: The Working Plan," *The Relaxation and Stress Reducing Workbook* (Oakland, CA: New Harbinger Publications, 1980), pp. 143–144.

2. *Identify situations in which you need to be more assertive.* Some of us are assertive at home, passive on the job, and aggressive when driving and shopping. We may also react differently to different people. For example, a person may be aggressive toward his or her spouse, assertive with the neighbors, and passive toward his or her own parents. Use the Situational Assertiveness Analysis Form in Figure 5.4 to help you determine the situations in which you need to be more assertive.

3. *Describe a typical situation in which assertiveness is a problem for you.* Who is involved? When and where does this situation take place? What specifically bothers you about the situation? How are you dealing with it now, and how would you like to deal with it? What is your goal for the interaction?

(continued on p. 95)

FIGURE 5.4
Situational Assertiveness Analysis Form

DIRECTIONS: Fill in each box, moving from left to right, using the following codes to indicate the frequency with which you engage in assertive behavior in each context:
1 = Usually
2 = Sometimes
3 = Seldom
NA = Not Applicable

FREQUENCY OF ASSERTIVENESS	Spouse	Child	Parents	Business contact	Authority figure	Same-sex friend	Opposite-sex friend	Co-workers	Neighbors	Students	Subordinates			
Giving compliments														
Receiving compliments														
Making requests														
Expressing liking, love, affection														
Standing up for rights														
Refusing requests														
Expressing personal opinion														
Expressing annoyance or displeasure														
Expressing anger														
Showing true emotions														
TOTALS:														

(Use blank columns for any additional contexts you wish to add.)

After filling out this assertiveness analysis form, you can study your own results to identify categories in which you might wish to be more assertive. For instance, you may find that while you are assertive with your parents you are passive with members of the opposite sex. You may find it easy to give compliments but difficult to refuse requests. Do you need to work on your assertiveness skills?

4. *Develop a working plan or script* for such a situation. Write down what you want to say and practice saying it. As time goes on and assertiveness skills are used more frequently, the steps will come more naturally and practice may not be necessary. (See "Developing the Working Plan: A Step-by-Step Approach" on page 93.)

5. *Develop assertive* **body language.** This includes such factors as good eye contact and posture; a clear, firm voice; and appropriate facial expressions.

6. *Avoid being manipulated* by the person you are confronting. Don't allow yourself to be sidetracked from the point you are trying to make and don't allow the interaction to degenerate into personal accusations.

As with other stress-management skills, learning to be assertive takes time and practice. If you think you need more help being assertive, check the resource list in the appendix of this book for suggestions.

Negative Self-Talk

Self-talk is the internal thinking process. It is mental feedback people give themselves as they carry on their daily activities. Much of this self-talk, unfortunately, is negative and can help create stress. [2]

For example, Bob asks his boss for a raise and is turned down. In denying Bob's request, his boss explains that there is not enough money in the budget at this time. Bob says to himself, "No wonder I can't get a raise. I am totally inferior to the other employees here. I am not a good person. The boss does not like me. I will never get promoted by this jerk." These responses evoke anxiety and depression and are a continual source of stress for Bob. Note that the boss's response did not cause the stress. Bob's irrational self-talk did. The boss merely said "not at this time." Everything else regarding inferior work, not being a good person, and not being liked by the boss originated in Bob's mind. Had Bob learned to control his irrational self-talk, he could have avoided a stress response.

The first step in changing negative self-talk is learning to identify it. When negative thoughts enter your mind, challenge them. Ask yourself what proof there is that your thinking is accurate. If it appears that you're engaging in negative self-talk, try to substitute more accurate and positive ideas. One good way to do this is to look for the positive things that have happened to

Body language: Gestures, mannerisms, and posture that communicate a person's disposition.

Harold has felt very reluctant to approach his boss to find out why he was turned down for a promotion. He's received no feedback about the reasons for the decision, and Harold is now feeling somewhat negative toward the company, and his boss in particular. Harold's script is as follows:

Look at: Resentment won't solve this. I need to assert my right to reasonable feedback from my employer.

Dealing With Negative Self-Talk: A Sample Working Plan

Arrange: I'll send him a memo tomorrow morning asking for time to discuss this problem.

Define: I haven't gotten any feedback about the promotion. The position I applied for has been filled by someone else, and that's all I know.

Describe: I felt uncomfortable not knowing at all why I didn't get it and how the decision was made.

Express: So I'd like to get some feedback from you about how my performance is seen, and what went into the decision.

Reinforce: I think your feedback will help me do a better job.

Source: M. Davis, E. R. Eshelman, M. McKay, "Assertiveness Training—Sample Working Plan," *The Relaxation and Stress Reduction Workbook* (Oakland, CA: New Harbinger Publications, 1980), p. 145.

you and dwell on them. From a stress-management perspective, it is better to err by being overly positive than by being too negative.

Type A Personality

An important perception-altering technique involves breaking out of Type A behaviors. Type A individuals tend to be very intense, ambitious, and competitive. They are often preoccupied with deadlines and feel pressure to attain a never-ending series of demanding personal and vocational goals. They work long hours at a fast pace and have few hobbies. They feel guilty when relaxing or taking time off from work. If you are a Type A person, chances are that your personality is a source of unnecessary stress.

If you are a Type A person, the following changes may help relieve stress: Learn to slow down—in working, eating, walking, and everything. Try to avoid doing more than one thing at a time and learn to relax without feeling guilty. Be patient when around

(continued on p. 100)

Change Your Type A Behavior

- Is "hurry up!" one of your most-used phrases?
- Do you look at your watch dozens of times a day?
- Do you think you have to do every job yourself, or else it's never going to get done right?
- Do you get equally upset by a lost glove as by your son's flunking English?
- Are you impatient, even hostile, when kept waiting or when delayed by an uncontrollable event, like a traffic jam?
- Do you constantly try to do more and more in less and less time, and then become anxious when it seems you can't meet all the deadlines?
- Do you find it impossible to say no when asked to assume a responsibility you don't want?
- Do you frequently accept social obligations you know you will resent?
- Are you spending less and less time with family and friends or on recreational activities?
- Are you a person with "high ideals" who is repeatedly disappointed when others don't live up to your standards?
- Do you often rush people's speech, finishing their sentences or saying "Yes, Yes," implying, "Get on with it!"?
- Do you get impatient and annoyed when you see people doing things you feel you can do faster or better?
- Do you have a hard time sitting and doing nothing?
- Do you often try to do or think of two or more things at once?
- Do you spend as much time and energy on trivial matters, or chores, as on important ones?

If you answered yes to more than half a dozen of these questions, then you're probably what psychologists and cardiologists call a "Type A" personality: a perfectionist—an idealistic, impatient, irritable victim of "hurry sickness." Type A people, research has shown, are especially prone to developing heart disease at an early age. But even if heart disease seems a distant or unlikely threat, being a full-fledged Type A personality is probably ruining the quality of your life, not to mention the lives of the people closest to you.

I know, because I used to be one: determined to be all things to all people; unwilling to say no, lest I be thought selfish, lazy or incompetent; unduly upset by every delayed plan; always pushing to be first; insistent that everything at home be done my way; impatient at work with anyone who did not catch on quickly. I was also chronically tense, hurried, irritable, and quick to fly into a rage. To me, life was a perpetual race, and I was determined to be the winner. Looking back on those years, I wonder how I managed to live with myself and how my husband put up with me.

Fortunately, he did, long enough for me to realize that some changes were desperately needed. My eyes were finally opened one day when I read a description of Type A people written by two San Francisco cardiologists, Dr. Meyer Friedman (himself a Type A heart attack victim) and Dr. Ray H. Rosenman. I recognized myself and I didn't like what I saw. Slowly, I began to make changes in my attitudes and actions, weaning myself from the more destructive and unpleasant parts of the Type A personality.

Now, more than five years later, I am still a Type A person, and like most other Type A's I wouldn't want to be otherwise. But having stepped off the tyrannical Type A treadmill, I am happier, more relaxed, and more appreciative of what life has to offer. I now enjoy my work a lot more, perhaps because I am better focused on what is really important, letting less-urgent matters wait (sometimes indefinitely), instead of constantly falling into a compulsion to do everything yesterday. I've actually become more productive.

How you can change Changing long-standing behavior and thought patterns does not happen overnight. It is a slow process, often with occasional setbacks that will remind you of how [entrenched] your Type A habits really are. But research has shown that habits are not irrevocable parts of your personality; any habit—whether it is twirling your hair around a finger, always getting angry in a particular situation, or simply chewing gum when you're feeling nervous—can be modified.

Changing habits starts with self-awareness and, unfortunately, Type A's generally deny there's anything wrong with how they act. It's the rest of the world that's wrong. Also, you might not be a full-blown, cardiac-prone Type A person but, rather, one who is only moderately afflicted. Still, there are undoubtedly characteristic behaviors and reactions you'd be happier shedding.

Learn to recognize your destructive attitude. The "fuel" for Type A behavior is a series of attitudes that govern your approach to life. They might include the following, and you're probably unaware of how they dominate you and those close to you:

* Your success depends not on quality but quantity: how much you can do or acquire.
* You are not really as good or successful as you want others to think; therefore, you must continually strive for the admiration of others.
* Your ideas of right and wrong are correct and not subject to modification.
* Life is competitive and demands fierce intent to win.
* Taking a breather, sitting quietly, or just "contemplating your navel" is wasteful.
* All activities must be done quickly and perfectly, or your world might collapse.

Revise your attitudes In contrast to the frenetic internal struggle of Type A's, so-called Type B people seem to have an inner tranquility. It comes from a sense of security and self-worth that needs no outside reinforcement. Type B people always feel they are doing their best, given their basic qualities. What others think is of no importance to them.

To emulate the Type B's of the world, then, Type A people need to realize that their frenzied pace practically guarantees eventual disaster in almost everything they do. They also need to be aware that their success thus far has not been because of their Type A behavior, but despite it. It's time to establish a new, more contemplative personality and a richer, less frenetic life. As Drs. Friedman and Rosenman point out in *Type A Behavior and Your Heart,* it's time to learn that "a

successful life is always unfinished." So begin your move from A to B with these steps:

* Stop measuring your life in quantities, whether it is the number of committees you're on or how many clients you serve. Shed some lesser obligations, such as memberships in organizations you care little about and tasks that serve only your vanity, rather than your spiritual or economic well-being. Whenever possible, turn over such tasks to other people or hire someone else to do them, especially if you don't really enjoy them. For example, I used to make most of my own clothes, but there are things other than tailoring I'd rather do with my time. So I now use a dressmaker, even to do such simple chores as hemming my skirts.
* Stop trying to be a [Superperson] who, in addition to having a demanding job, insists on controlling everything at home. . . . Forget about perfection: you will not be judged unworthy because there's some dust on the piano or the sheets are not folded perfectly. Anyone who does judge you on that basis is not worth having as a friend. Delegate some responsibilities to others in the family. For example, my sons now wash nearly all the dishes, and my husband does most of the grocery shopping, which gives me more time to cook, something I enjoy and that is important to my career.
* Learn how to say no when asked to take on an unwanted responsibility. I've had a much easier time doing this ever since I realized it was a symptom of my insecurity to think I must do whatever was asked of me.
* Start cultivating your spiritual side (even though you might not know you have one). Buy tickets to a concert or play, walk through a park once or twice a week, cultivate a friendship, read a book for pleasure. Think of these activities as soul-restoring and life-enhancing, not as squandering time that could be used to "accomplish" something.
* Learn to enjoy the unexpected. Instead of treating every unplanned event as a disruption from your main tasks, allow yourself some flexibility. You'll be pleasantly surprised.

Slowing your pace Cure your "hurry" sickness. For too many Type A people, life is quite literally a race to the death. Yet, the sense of urgency is one of [the] easiest—and most rewarding—Type A characteristics to modify. I know, because it's one I have worked hardest on, and the resulting reduction in stress and the improvement in quality of life has been its own reward. Here's how to go about making this change:

• Allow extra time to get somewhere or do something. Then, if you are unavoidably delayed, you can still reach your destination without becoming unduly anxious.

• Always carry something to read or do with your hands, in case you have to wait around or stand in line. You'll be less likely to become overly tense about "wasting" time. If you're caught without anything to do, strike up a conversation with a stranger or spend the time daydreaming (daydreams can sometimes be constructive).

• Don't schedule every minute of every day, every day of every week, and every week of every year with activities and appointments, and don't create unnecessary deadlines. For example, whenever possible say, "I'll be there between 11:00 and 11:30," rather than, "See you at 11:00 sharp."

• Even when working against a deadline, take periodic breaks. Walk around, talk to a friend, stare out the window, get some exercise; anything to relieve the tension. Chances are, when you get back to work you'll be more efficient.

• End the morning "rush hour" by getting up 15 or 30 minutes earlier. Your body and mind will get far more benefit from a leisurely start of the day than from those extra minutes of sleep.

• Sort your day's chores (and mail) into "must do today," "can wait a day or two," and "can wait indefinitely." And don't fret about the last category. Nothing terrible will happen if you don't get to those chores.

• Leave your watch home for a day, then try leaving it behind for two or three days. You might find after a while that you hardly ever need it.

Toning down your temper Conquer your hostility. Quickness to anger is the most self-destruc-

tive of the Type A characteristics, the one most closely linked to the development of heart disease. It is also the trait that makes Type A people so unpleasant to live and work with. Take an inventory of the situations that typically anger or annoy you, and start using your mind and sense of humor to get you through. Be on guard for particular "angry areas":

• Avoid people who always "get to you." As for annoying relatives and co-workers you must see from time to time, let them do all the talking. Don't rise to their bait, and don't try to defend yourself when they attack. Just pretend to listen, and keep your mind on something more pleasant.

• Save your anger for the few situations that really count, such as when someone deliberately hurts you. Don't waste anger on trivia or on matters you cannot control, such as the slowness of the mail or the pokiness of a salesperson.

• Don't regard the aggressive or hostile actions of others as a deliberate personal affront. The driver who passes you, the person who pushes ahead of you in line, the passerby who litters your walk, would do the same to anyone.

• Stop focusing on your "ideals" and noticing how many people fall short of them. There is no one correct way to live, any more than there is a single correct religion. Instead of being hostile, try to be more understanding, tolerant and affectionate.

• Cultivate a friendship with a Type B person. He or she can serve as model of the behavior you are aiming toward.

• After making even some of the changes listed above, you are likely to find that you're doing less, but enjoying life a great deal more. And as an added bonus, you'll discover you've made important strides toward becoming the type of person others are pleased to share the world with.

Source: Jane Brody, "Improve Your Health—Change Your Type A Behavior," *Family Circle* (May 1984).

less ambitious Type B individuals and feel compassion, not competition, for other Type As. Work on your powers of concentration; perhaps you could read a book that requires attention and patience. Set your priorities each morning and plan each day accordingly. The goal here is not to become less productive but to become more selectively productive and to do so in a way that is realistic and less conducive to stress. Making these changes is not easy, but with time and effort, it can be done.

STRESS-RELIEVING PERSONALITY TRAITS

Just as there are personality traits that tend to make a person more susceptible to stress, there are traits one can cultivate to help relieve potentially stressful situations.

Humor

Humor in and of itself does not qualify as a comprehensive stress-management program, but learning to take things less seriously and including laughter in one's life can certainly be one component of stress control.

The notion that laughter feels good and helps us to relax is not a new one. Proverbs 17:22 (King James Version) reminds us that "A merry heart doeth good like a medicine." For years *Reader's Digest* has run a monthly feature entitled "Laughter Is the Best Medicine." It was not, however, until Norman Cousins wrote his best-selling book, *Anatomy of an Illness,* proclaiming the benefits of laughter in his recovery from a normally progressive and crippling spinal disease, that people began believing that laughter has some therapeutic value. [3] Given the potential value of humor, it makes sense to put it to work in our lives. Start looking for the absurd and silly activities that go on around you and do not be afraid to laugh at them.

Androgyny

The term **androgyny** may bring to mind rock stars who appear to be ambivalent about their gender. In truth, the word stems from the two Greek roots: "andro" meaning male, and "gyn" meaning female. Therefore, androgyny refers to the combining of stereotypical male and female traits.

Everyone, regardless of gender, has both male and female traits. A blending of the two sets of traits allows a person to be both self-reliant and compassionate and to function more effec-

Androgyny: The state of having a combination of both male and female qualities and characteristics.

(continued on p. 102)

Laughter as Potential Therapy

"A merry heart doeth good like a medicine," it says in Proverbs, 17:22. Similarly, *Reader's Digest* reminds us monthly, "Laughter is the best medicine."

Can these popular sources of wisdom be wrong? Not at all, say a growing number of physicians, nurses, psychologists and patients who have used this uniquely human expression of mirth to reduce stress, ease pain, foster recovery and generally brighten one's outlook on life, regardless of how grim the reality.

Their interest in the therapeutic potential of laughter was largely spurred by the publicized recovery of the editor Norman Cousins from a usually progressive, crippling spinal disease, ankylosing spondylitis. He said his recovery was facilitated by self-prescribed daily doses of humor.

Several hospitals and nursing homes have recently begun to send around laughter wagons stocked with joke books, humorous tapes, toys, games and other gimmicks likely to amuse patients. A few hospitals have set up "humor rooms" where patients and their families can join staff members for a hearty laugh stimulated by funny videos, joke telling and live performances, sometimes by the patients themselves.

The nuns at St. Joseph's Hospital in Houston are required to tell each patient a funny story every day. At Oregon Health Sciences University, members of a local group, Nurses for Laughter, wear buttons that read: "Warning: Humor may be hazardous to your illness." And growing numbers of cancer patients are participating in laughter therapy groups that help ease the burden of the disease and possibly foster recovery.

While it is hard to find health professionals who are against laughter, at least as an adjunct to modern medical care, it is also hard to find scientific evidence for its therapeutic value. Anecdotes abound along the lines of Mr. Cousins's remarkable recovery after doses of Laurel and Hardy, the Marx Brothers and old "Candid Camera" clips.

As Mr. Cousins reported in his bestselling book, "Anatomy of an Illness," just 20 minutes of hearty laughing bought him two hours of painless sleep, with no unwanted side effects. Tests showed that after each laugh session his crippling inflammation subsided a bit. He likened laughing's physiological and psychological effects to "internal jogging," a kind of sedentary aerobic exercise.

Physiological Effects

Dr. William F. Fry, a psychiatrist affiliated with Stanford University who has been a student of laughter for three decades, said that laughing 100 times a day is equivalent to about 10 minutes of rowing. He says laughter stimulates the production of the alertness hormones catecholamines. These hormones in turn cause the release of endorphins in the brain. Endorphins foster a sense of relaxation and well-being and dull the perception of pain.

Catecholamines also enhance blood flow and thus may speed healing, reduce inflammation and stimulate alertness. There is also some preliminary evidence that laughter enhances the immune response by reducing hormones that suppress immunity.

As Dr. Marvin E. Herring, a family practitioner at New Jersey's School of Osteopathic Medicine, puts it, "The diaphragm, thorax, abdomen, heart, lungs and even the liver are given a massage during a hearty laugh."

Most obvious, however, are laughter's effects on cardiovascular and respiratory functions. When one is laughing hard, normal breathing rhythm is disrupted. Inhalation and expiration become more spasmodic as well as deeper. Heart rate, blood pressure and muscular tension increase, but when laughter subsides, these levels often drop temporarily to below normal, leaving one very relaxed. Hence the expression "weak with laughter" to describe someone who has just laughed hard and long.

This sense of relaxation lasts about 45 minutes after the last laugh, and may be beneficial in countering heart disease, high blood pressure and depression. Given these benefits, proponents of laughter therapy jokingly call it "ho-ho-holistic medicine."

Put Laughter to Work

Few students of laughter would suggest relying on it to the exclusion of traditional medicine. Similarly, few traditional therapists would spurn the contribution of laughter. How, then, can laughter be put to work as a healer?

• Instead of flowers, consider sending the patient a funny novel, a book of jokes, a silly toy, a humorous audio tape and portable recorder or, if a video recorder is available, a funny movie. When my best friend contracted a life-threatening disease, I made her a loose-leaf "book of laughs" stuffed with New Yorker cartoons, classic witticisms and personalized homemade jokes. Years after recovering, she continues to use the joke book whenever she thinks she is getting sick.

• Brighten the sick room with mobiles, homemade silly sculptures, comical photos and get-well cards. Place a poster of a scenic view on the window or wall and change it often.

• Keep on the lookout for humorous happenings and statements that you can tell the patient about. Arrive at the bedside with a funny story instead of a complaint about the terrible traffic or the parking problem.

• Seek out caretakers with a sense of humor. Dianne-Jo Moore, writing in *Aimplus,* a magazine for the Arthritis Foundation, tells of her 69-year-old mother's preoperative experience. When the orderly arrived to take the tense, anxious woman to the operating room, he announced with a nod toward the stretcher, "I have my limousine just outside your door, and I'm here to give you curbside service." Her mother's tension, indeed the whole family's, dissolved in the warmth of his humor.

• Consider organizing a local scout troop, school or senior citizens group to prepare riddles or jokes that can be placed on patients' breakfast trays. Or challenge patients to come up with their own humorous captions for cartoon drawings.

. . . It is also appropriate to consider how you can foster your own sense of well-being by various measures to increase your "laugh-ability." Dr. Joel Goodman, director of the Humor Project at Sagamore Institute in Saratoga Springs, N.Y., recommends the following:

• Start looking for the absurd, silly, incongruous activities that go on around you.

• Take a 5- to 10-minute humor break each day. Read jokes, add to a humor notebook, listen to a funny tape, play with a small child.

• Practice "tongue-fu," a verbal form of martial art. Prepare quick retorts and creative punch lines to disarm predictable verbal attacks. When the humorist Robert Benchley asked a uniformed man outside a restaurant to hail him a cab, the man snapped, "I happen to be a rear admiral in the United States Navy." Mr. Benchley's swift response: "O.K., then, get me a battleship."

• Avoid sarcasm and ridicule. Concentrate on esteem-building humor, not quips that are self-degrading or demeaning to others.

Finally, when you hear a good joke, write it down or quickly relate it to someone to help you remember it.

Source: Jane Brody, *New York Times,* 7 April 1988, Sec. 2, p. 8.

tively in everyday life. Studies indicate that developing an androgynous personality can lead to a less stressful life-style. [4]

Acquiring such a personality is not synonymous with abandoning one's masculinity or femininity. A man can still exhibit traditional masculine traits while incorporating into his personality traits often considered feminine, such as tenderness, recep-

FIGURE 5.5
Laughter

Laughter is a workout for the body; after a hearty laugh heart rate, blood pressure, and muscular tension drop below their normal levels, leaving a person feeling very relaxed. Laughter may also stimulate the release by the brain of substances called endorphins that both relieve pain and ease anxiety.

tivity, and nurturing toward others. He can allow himself to become more human and to express feelings he would normally suppress, such as sadness accompanied by tears. Many men watch a sensitive, tender movie and feel they must hold back the tears because they believe that it is not masculine to cry. This holding back of emotions may contribute to stress-related illnesses for men in our society.

Women, on the other hand, can still express feminine traits while at the same time adopting traditional masculine behaviors such as assertiveness and forcefulness. Women can accept leadership roles and take more responsibility in decision-making. In the past these traits have frequently been suppressed by women, resulting in feelings of inferiority and frustration. In women, as in men, suppressing the positive traits traditionally assigned to the opposite sex causes stress.

Androgyny broadens our repertoire of available behaviors, which in turn creates a sense of balance that can help us cope with stress at home, at school, or on the job.

SUMMARY

Perception and personality traits play a critical role in creating and relieving stress. Although it may seem more effective to reduce stress by altering the surrounding environment rather than by altering your own perceptions and personalities, such is not always the case.

You can do a great deal to eliminate counterproductive personality traits and to encourage helpful ones. Procrastination is a damaging personality trait you can overcome through dedication, self-discipline, and careful planning. Assertiveness training can make your interactions with others more positive. Negative self-talk is highly stressful, but learning to spot it, and to challenge the rationality of your mental statements, can help you focus more on the positive in your life. If you have a Type A personality, you can work at becoming more relaxed and less driven. Perhaps most important, learn techniques that help make potentially stressful situations less difficult. Laugh as much as you can; it will relax you and help you gain perspective on some issues that don't have to be taken seriously. At the same time, don't stop yourself from crying if a situation calls for it. Expressing your feelings honestly and openly is one of the most physically and emotionally healthy things you can do for yourself. W

Modifying the Stress Response

ELIZABETH WRIGHT works full-time as an administrative assistant in a corporation, is married, and has a son in the third grade. Two years ago, her many responsibilities as employee, wife, and mother were putting her in an almost continuous state of stress. When she went to her doctor complaining of severe headaches, he advised her to do something to reduce her stress level.

After careful research, Elizabeth devised a plan that included time management, assertiveness, and nutrition. She rearranged her work schedule to make more efficient use of her time, she asked her husband to take on more of the household and parenting tasks, and she started drinking decaffeinated instead of regular coffee and eating 3 balanced meals each day. These steps eliminated much of her stress, but not all of it. There are times when stress is unavoidable on her job—for example, when she must prepare the annual report on a strict deadline. Since she cannot eliminate all the stress itself, Elizabeth does the next best thing. She takes steps to control her reaction to stress.

This chapter will review the third part of a comprehensive stress-management program: finding ways to minimize the stress reaction once it occurs. This step is essential, since most of us will experience some stress even when we take steps to reduce stressors and control stress-inducing personality factors. Techniques such as exercise, meditation, progressive relaxation, autogenic training, and biofeedback have all proved successful in minimizing the stress reaction.

(continued on p. 107)

The Art of Relaxation

It is surprising how little Americans know about the art of relaxation. Relaxation is more than getting away from the work-a-day grind, and it is more than the absence of stress. It is something positive and satisfying—a feeling in which one experiences peace of mind. True relaxation requires becoming sensitive to one's basic needs for peace, self-awareness, thoughtful reflection—and the willingness to meet these needs rather than ignoring or dismissing them.

The continuing pressures of everyday life take a heavy toll on the physical and mental well-being of millions of people each year. Medical research into the origins of common diseases such as high blood pressure, heart disease, ulcers, and headaches shows a connection between stress and the development of such ailments. In the area of mental health, stress frequently underlies emotional and behavioral problems, including nervous breakdowns. Various environmental factors—from noise and air pollution to economic disruptions, such as unemployment, inflation, and recession—can make living conditions even more stressful. These conditions, in turn, can create a greater need for mental health services to help people cope more effectively with their environment.

In the course of a day, people are frequently distracted from their activities by personal problems—conflicts with family members, disagreements with employers, poor living or working conditions, boredom, loneliness—to name just a few. It is easy to get so preoccupied with living, thinking, organizing, existing, and working that a person disregards his or her needs for relaxation.

More people reared in our production-oriented society feel guilty, or at least ill-at-ease, when they are not actively involved in accomplishing tasks or producing things. Even their vacations become whirlwind productions that leave the participants exhausted after concentrating too many experiences into a short period of time. Such behavior undermines the value of vacation time as an opportunity for diversion, calm, resto-ration of one's energies, and gaining new experiences.

Secret of Relaxation

Unfortunately, some people pursue relaxation with the same concern for time, productivity, and activity that they show in their everyday life patterns. Far too few people know how to turn off their body clocks and gain satisfaction out of just being instead of always striving. The secret in getting the best results from attempts at relaxation is simple: Find those activities which give you pleasure, and, when you pursue them, commit your energies to total mental and physical well-being. If your diversion results in an artistic product, musical skills, further education, a better physique, or whatever, that's great. But remember that relaxation, not achievement, is your main reason for participating in the activity.

Mental health specialists have come up with some suggestions for learning the art of relaxation:

Try Something New and Different

Keep in mind two important rules of thumb in deciding on relaxation activities: Do not be afraid to try something new and different. Choose activities you really enjoy, not activities you think other people want you to pursue. The following are some activities worth thinking about:

1. Check out various community activities available through recreation departments, adult education programs, volunteer work opportunities, college courses, etc.

2. Consider exercise such as walking around your neighborhood or in the woods, and bicycling, dancing, playing golf, swimming, gardening, bowling, etc.

3. For the more physically fit, more strenuous exercise can prove most relaxing. Jogging, playing tennis, basketball, handball, squash, etc., can give one a feeling of wonderful relaxation after an intense workout.

4. Try some mental exercises to create a sense of peace and tranquility in body and mind. One such exercise involves concentration on relaxing successive sets of muscles from the tips of your toes to the muscles in your forehead and neck. Other mental relaxation techniques include getting fully involved with a good book, drifting off into a quiet state with music, or focusing on a beautiful scene or drawing and losing oneself in it.

5. Creative activities such as painting, drawing, pottery, carpentry, knitting, and even cooking for fun, can also give you a sense of accomplishment, as well as the peaceful relaxation of concentration on something you wish to do.

6. Whether or not the above suggestions for relaxation work in your case, a surefire method known down through the ages is the use of a warm bath to take away bodily stress and strain. You may choose to enhance this activity by reading a good book, listening to music, or even adding some bubbles if you like.

Practice Relaxation Daily

After discovering your favorite relaxation activity, plan to devote at least one-half hour per day to pursuing it. Most people accept the responsibility to meet deadlines and duties imposed on them by others, but it is equally important for them to meet the requirements for relaxation periods demanded by their own minds and bodies. Hard-working homemakers or busy executives must give themselves opportunities for relaxation if they are to maintain their mental balance through stressful events and hectic schedules.

Making a Personal Commitment

The third and final principle in the art of relaxation is to enter into relaxation activities with enthusiasm and personal commitment. Let yourself become completely involved in the relaxation activity chosen; do not hold back physically or mentally.

Remember, finding effective techniques for personal relaxation is not merely a pastime for the idle rich. It is essential for everyone's physical and mental well-being.

—*Louis E. Kopolow, M.D.*

Source: Department of Health and Human Services, HHS Publication No. (ADM) 85–632, 1985.

PHYSICAL ACTIVITY

The purpose of the stress response has always been to prepare the human body for physical exertion—fight or flight. As previously mentioned, fight and flight are usually inappropriate responses in today's society, since stressors tend to be sociological or psychological in nature. The stress response can, therefore, leave a person in a state of heightened physical arousal but without a proper outlet for release. One good solution to this problem is daily exercise.

There are many different kinds of exercise, and different kinds appeal to different individuals. Some people enjoy competitive sports, such as tennis, racketball, and handball. These can be

FIGURE 6.1
Combating Stress with Physical Activity

Exercise is an excellent stress reliever. But when playing a competitive sport, such as volleyball, it's important to keep winning or losing the game from becoming a source of stress.

Circulatory system: The system consisting of the heart and blood vessels that maintains the flow of blood throughout the body.

excellent stress relievers as long as participants can disengage their egos. In other words, if they can feel relaxed and refreshed after a match even when they lose, their stress is being reduced. If, however, losing results in feelings of anger and frustration that persist for a considerable time after the activity, such activities may actually increase stress.

Individual cardiovascular exercises, such as walking, jogging, cycling, and swimming are good choices, for they not only provide an outlet for the stress response but also help condition the heart, lungs, and **circulatory system**. These activities usually do not involve ego unless the participant engages in them competitively or sets unrealistic individual goals. In addition, everyone, regardless of conditioning level, can participate. Even those who are completely out of shape can begin a walking program.

(continued on p. 110)

Sweat Your Worries Away?

Diehard exercisers often preach the gospel that exercise helps you manage stress. So far, research has shown that people are often relaxed in the afterglow of a single aerobic workout. But there's less evidence that exercising regularly leads to a lasting reduction in stress.

Tension eases for several hours after an aerobic workout, regardless of how fit you are. In a series of studies beginning in the 1960's, University of Southern California researcher Herbert deVries, Ph.D., tested that "tranquilizer effect." Using an electrical measure of muscle tension, deVries has found that such rhythmic exercises as walking, jogging, and bicycling decrease tension—by as much as nearly 60 percent for up to 90 minutes.

Exercise can also lower blood pressure, another physical sign some researchers use to gauge stress. A 1987 study showed that either aerobic exercise or quiet rest for about 40 minutes lowered blood pressure and eased feelings of anxiety. But blood pressure stayed low for less than half an hour after resting, compared with two to three hours after exercising.

In this and other studies, feelings of anxiety were measured with the State-Trait Anxiety Inventory. It asks you to respond to statements such as "I feel calm" by choosing an answer ranging from "not at all" to "very much so." A 1987 review of seven studies using the Inventory showed consistent drops in anxiety after an aerobic workout.

But short-term exercise is only a short-term fix. "Individuals may escape the daily pressure of their jobs, home, or school environments by taking time out to engage in vigorous physical activity," wrote researcher David R. Brown, Ph.D., of Miami University of Ohio, in a 1988 review article. "However, within two to five hours after returning to the environment from which they escaped, the psychological benefits . . . are lost."

What about the long run?

Whether regular exercise confers a more lasting reduction in stress is less clear. A regimen of aerobic exercise does have lasting cardiovascular benefits, including drops in heart rate and blood pressure. But what about subjective measures? Does regular exercise make you feel less "stressed out" over the long haul?

Reasoning that exercise is itself a form of stress, researchers have speculated that regular exercise may act like a "stress vaccine," making you more resistant at least to brief periods of stress in your life. They've tested this notion by observing people who exercise and people who don't as they face mental stress from an arithmetic test, for example. The results have been mixed.

In a 1987 overview of 34 conflicting studies, researchers concluded that fit people may indeed be stress resistant. Since then, the researchers have finished an unpublished overview of 104 studies—including the original 34—that reaches the same conclusion.

But that conclusion may rest on shaky underpinnings. In many of the studies considered in both overviews, participants were not randomly assigned to either exercise or sedentary groups. Researchers merely observed stress responses in people who were categorized according to their fitness levels. So exercisers may have responded better to stress because of inherent physical or psychological differences between people who choose to exercise and those who don't.

Moreover, those studies focused on temporary, isolated stresses. They didn't measure the effects of regular exercise on chronic stress—say, that experienced by an air traffic controller. Only a few studies have assigned people to exercise or no-exercise groups and then tested how they deal with chronic stress. A 1989 study reported the benefits of exercise in men who learned they were infected with the AIDS virus. "I can't think of a more powerful stressor," University of Miami researcher Arthur LaPerriere, Ph.D., told CRHL [*Consumer Reports Health Letter*].

LaPerriere randomly split 46 apparently healthy, gay men into two groups: One performed aerobic exercise three times a week for 10 weeks; the other didn't exercise. At the start, the men didn't know whether they were infected; in fact, 24 of them were. After they found out, five weeks into the study, LaPerriere measured the men's physical and psychological reactions. Immediately after receiving the news, all 24 infected men were extremely anxious. But a week later, the 14 infected men who had been exercising felt significantly calmer than the 10 who hadn't exercised. In fact, their scores on the State-Trait Anxiety Inventory and other tests resembled those of the noninfected men.

Which workout works?

So far, most research showing a temporary reduction in stress after a workout has focused on aerobic exercise. Two studies in the 1970's found that nonaerobic exercise did not significantly affect the subjects' perceptions of stress. On the other hand, even light, nonaerobic exercise such as walking has been shown to ease muscle tension.

Both aerobic and nonaerobic exercise share certain qualities—an enhanced sense of control or achievement, "time out" from everyday concerns, or even the chance to socialize—that may relieve stress in some people.

"But even if the benefit comes from the distraction or the sense of control," LaPerriere told CRHL, "exercise is still an effective tool for managing stress." And, of course, exercise also has other health benefits.

If you do try exercising to manage stress, keep in mind that a workout probably won't do much good if it's unpleasant. Try not to spend the whole session worrying about taking the time from your busy schedule. Choose an exercise that won't create new aggravations.

"If you're overweight," notes Cornell University researcher Michael Sacks, M.D., "doing aerobics at a **health spa** with a bunch of people in tights may not be the most effective form of stress reduction." But going for a long walk in a peaceful setting might.

Source: *Consumer Reports Health Letter,* May 1990, pp. 36–37.

Activities such as aerobic dance and yoga relieve stress efficiently. These activities are both body-awareness activities. This means that they force the mind to concentrate on the body's movement and, in the process, let go of stressful thoughts because the mind cannot focus on two things at once.

For some people, the thought of exercise is stressful. They may have had negative experiences with exercise in the past and are reluctant to try again. These individuals need extra support and encouragement to get involved in a regular exercise program.

It is important to select the right time to initiate your exercise program. As a general rule, it is probably better not to initiate it during a period of high stress. At such times, people often feel overloaded already, so adding another activity is not realistic. It is better to pick a period of low stress. If that is not possible, however, exercise should be started on a gradual basis

Health spa: An often luxurious, residential, resortlike facility operated on a commercial basis that offers a variety of health-related services.

(continued on p. 112)

Yoga: Stressless Exercises

Yoga's image problem is largely undeserved—you aren't expected to sit motionless for hours or to force your body into painful positions. But it isn't hard to see why many Westerners are wary of yoga if you've heard about some of the more advanced practices, such as *vastra dhauti,* in which one slowly swallows a fifteen-foot strip of gauze cloth and then pulls it back out of the stomach through the mouth in the hope that unnecessary mucus and bodily waste will cling to it. Stack that up against relaxation techniques like watching TV or getting a massage, and yoga will come out last almost every time.

But yoga is supposed to be good for relieving stress, so I went to classes at the Lotus Yoga Center, which is really the Silver Spring apartment of Riki Middleton, who has been teaching yoga for nineteen years. She also teaches classes in meditation and vegetarian nutrition and leads a yoga-and-diet retreat in the country each spring and fall.

When I arrived for class on a Saturday morning, she and five students were sitting on white sheets spread on her living room floor. The students, four women and one man, were all fidgeting in one way or another, but Middleton sat calmly in the famous lotus position, the one that twelve-year-old girls use for séances, and told me to make myself comfortable near her on the floor.

For the next hour and a half, Middleton guided us through a series of relaxation techniques and yoga "poses" that stretched and exercised different muscles. Unlike the exercises most of us learned in kindergarten—the jumping jacks, sit-ups, push-ups—yoga doesn't involve rapid, repetitive motions or straining. Instead, the body is conditioned by various positions that are arrived at gently and held for fifteen seconds or longer.

First we lay on our backs with our arms at our sides and palms up—the corpse pose—then we lifted our arms up and let them fall back over our heads. We stretched our right sides, then our left sides, then both sides at once. We pulled our legs onto our chests while lifting our heads to stretch our backs, we rolled our necks slowly from side to side, we stretched our lower lips over our upper lips, which looks awful but feels good. We did the cobra, lying on our stomachs and raising our heads and chests, which is good for the abdominal muscles and back; we assumed the turtle pose, sitting with our legs spread, upper torsos forward and down, and arms placed forward underneath the legs. Our thighs and groins were well stretched.

True to my preconceptions about yoga teachers, Middleton seems to radiate serenity. But she led us through the exercises with a decided intensity. She is tall and slender, almost bony, but she moves into and out of the positions with a striking lightness and grace.

I was the only rank beginner in the class, and she took care to show me how to perform the exercises without overstretching. It isn't necessary to push yourself to the limits of your flexibility; the positions are supposed to *not* hurt. If you are from the no-pain-no-gain school of recreation, you are going to have to deprogram yourself for yoga. Yoga calls for gentle stretching; by repeating the poses over time and adding more advanced ones, you tone your muscles and increase flexibility.

At the end of the session we all lay on our backs again, eyes closed, and Middleton talked us through a limb-by-limb relaxation routine to the accompaniment of soft music. That was it. There was no chanting, no praying.

The 5,000-year-old corpus of yogic principles embodies the bodily positions—thousands of them—and a philosophy of human purpose that encompasses moral values, diet, reincarnation, the nature of reality, and our relationship with God. But even long-time practitioners agree that there is nothing wrong with taking a few good things from yoga and, if you choose, leaving the rest behind.

Once you know what you are doing, you can practice yoga almost anywhere, without special clothing or equipment—at home, at your office, traveling on business. If you aren't worried about looking weird, you can do *simhasana,* the lion pose, while in line at the bank—stick your tongue out as far as it will go and roll your eyes all the way up.

What about yoga and stress? Almost anything you do that gets you breathing more deeply and gets your body into better shape will make you feel better both mentally and physically. A good yoga teacher will also help you address specific problems—a sore back, daily headaches, chronic insomnia. But as with any technique, a lot depends on your attitude, because the physical poses alone are not going to *make* you relax. Good yoga teachers emphasize the importance of correct breathing, which in yoga is slow and deliberate and timed to coincide with movement. It takes some discipline and concentration, but if you do it right, you almost can't help feeling better.

Source: Steven D. Kaye, *The Washingtonian* (February 1989), p. 128.

even during a high-stress period. A 5-minute walk down the hall at lunchtime, for instance, can be expanded over time to a 20-minute walk 4 to 5 days a week. Constant time demands and high stress levels are not good excuses for delaying the start of an exercise program.

Once exercise has been initiated, however, it becomes an important outlet during any high-stress period. Unfortunately, many people are tempted to drop their exercise programs during times of stress. Students, for example, often exercise faithfully during the term, only to stop at exam time. Exercise needs to be given as high a priority as eating and sleeping. During a period of high stress, exercise should be the last thing to be cut, not the first.

On the other hand, it is important not to become addicted to exercise. Some people enter an exercise program and become so enthusiastic that they go overboard. This is particularly likely to occur among competitive, highly stressed, Type A individuals. These people may want to become marathon runners after training for only a month. Moreover, unless exercise is approached properly and increased gradually, injuries can occur, which then become another source of stress. Furthermore, some people spend so much time training that it becomes a drain on their time and increases stress in their personal or professional lives.

In addition to injuries and time problems, overdoing exercise may actually increase one's risk of cancer. Preliminary studies conducted by Dr. Leonard Cohen, a biologist at the Naylor Dana Institute for Disease Prevention in Valhalla, New York, have indicated that the protective element of exercise disappears with higher levels of exercise. [1] After examining the development of both mammary tumors and colon cancer in rats, Cohen and his fellow researchers determined that exercise not only reduced the number of tumors but also delayed their onset. Among the most active groups of rats, however, this protection disappeared, and these animals had tumor levels comparable to their nonexercising counterparts. While it is too early to determine if exercise affects humans in the same way, this is certainly a line of research to watch in the future. With exercise, as with all activities, moderation is probably the best policy.

MEDITATION

In everyday life, we direct most of our mental activity outward. We develop and solve problems, analyze, synthesize, plan, communicate, interact, and much more. Seldom, however, do we get in touch with our inner selves. Seldom do we quiet our bodies and minds so that we can listen to and feel what is going on inside. Meditation teaches people how to do this. It allows the meditator to focus uncritically on one thing at a time. Because this skill can then be applied to other areas of life, it allows people to concentrate better and focus on whatever they are doing.

Meditation also produces a state of deep relaxation in a relatively short period of time. The body's metabolism slows down as oxygen consumption, carbon dioxide production, respiration rate, heart rate, and blood pressure all decrease. Meditation increases the amount of **alpha brain waves**, which result from a state of deep relaxation. It has been suggested that this state of deep relaxation is the result of focusing the mind on only one thing; thus, the amount of internal and external stimuli one must respond to is greatly lessened.

The best place to meditate is somewhere quiet and free of the hustle and bustle of daily living. First find a comfortable sitting position you can maintain for 20 minutes without tiring. This may entail sitting cross-legged on the floor, Japanese fashion on the knees with big toes touching and heels pointing outward so that the buttocks rest on the feet, in the traditional yoga **lotus position,** or on a chair with arms and legs resting in a relaxed manner. It is important to sit straight with the weight of the head centered directly over the spinal column.

Next, choose an object on which to concentrate. This is either a word or a sound you can say, either aloud or to yourself. In some forms of meditation, the meditator has his or her own word or

Alpha brain waves: Brain waves that occur at an average of 10 waves per second, characteristic of a relaxed state.

Lotus position: A meditating position in which one sits on the floor with knees bent, ankles crossed, and hands joined.

FIGURE 6.2
Meditation

Meditation produces a state of deep relaxation in a relatively short period of time. The body's metabolism slows as breathing, heart rate, and blood pressure all decrease.

mantra, while in others any word will work. While you are meditating, maintain a receptive attitude. Clear all thoughts and distractions from your mind. If you find yourself thinking about something, try to stop or else acknowledge it gently, then mentally put it aside to think about later. In addition, don't be concerned with how well you are meditating. Self-criticism tends to interfere with the goals of meditation.

Besides improving concentration, meditation has been shown to help prevent and treat hypertension, strokes, and heart disease. It can also be a good way to cope with anxiety, depression, and hostility and to curtail obsessive thinking. [2]

Mantra: A word or a sound that can be thought, imagined, or spoken during meditation.

(continued on p. 116)

It was late in 1983 and the weasels were closing in. I was a late-blooming reporter at a weekly newspaper in Howard County—chasing cops and robbers, rummaging through court files, angling for story quota, working marathon hours, and mainlining five coffees a day in a routinely failing quest for the deadline.

It would sometimes be like this through the weekend. Friends gave up. My girlfriend ditched me. Insomnia reigned. My mind would clog with information overload.

Transcendental Meditation: "Restful Alertness"

The hammer came down when my high blood pressure went out of control, threatening a stroke at the age of 26. I'd get blinding migraines once a month. Something had to give.

A Colorado friend had been intimating for months that transcendental meditation was a proven drug-free treatment for high blood pressure. He showed me the trick during a five-day hike through the Canyonlands of Utah. He taught me how to say a two-syllable mantra in my mind for twenty minutes, twice a day. It was kind of fun.

There are long-established mantras, all words without specific meaning, handed down from ancient India and said to possess a special harmonic quality that settles the mind. The words are kept secret, so that those seeking to practice TM must go through the proper training.

My morning routine starts by sitting quietly with my eyes closed. I clear my head for 30 seconds, and then begin repeating the mantra in my mind in a slow and natural rhythm. It becomes automatic and easy after the first few lessons. The pace of the mantra reminds me of water lapping at the edge of a lake in a light wind.

Sometimes the last song on the clock radio plays back in my mind even as I hear the mantra, and other thoughts always come and go. But the end result is that my mind is clearer after meditating.

My evening routine is similar, except that I often do it while taking the train home. To an outside observer it looks only like I'm taking a nap.

Five years later I'm still doing the routine, my blood pressure is under control, and I can't remember the last time I had a migraine. The weasels have stopped closing in.

There's some science behind all of this. TM people like to point to the 1971 "Wallace-Benson" study, performed jointly at Harvard Medical School and the University of California. It found that TM practitioners could slip into a state now widely called "restful alertness," where involuntary bodily functions would slow significantly more than even in deep sleep, but the mind would be awake.

Brain waves and breathing slowed. Heart rates would decrease an average of three beats a minute. Basal skin resistance—where skin becomes drier and less conducive to electrical current—would increase fourfold, indicating deep relaxation.

Some studies show, after weeks or months of practicing TM, an average reduction of both **systolic** and **diastolic** blood pressure by ten points each.

Other studies also show increases in clarity of thinking, academic performance, creativity, general health, and longevity.

That TM's clinical benefits in stress-reduction have been verified shouldn't hide the fact that it is first and foremost a spiritual technique. While proponents deny there is any formal belief system attached to TM, claims of tapping into the "unified field" to promote world peace require a leap of faith. For me the jury's still out.

In any case, a recent call to one of the Harvard study's authors supported one of my pet suspicions: The TM technique doesn't have exclusive rights to the clinical benefits of meditation. "There are scores of ways to elicit the 'relaxation response' " sought in meditation, says Harvard Medical School associate professor Dr. Herbert Benson, who makes a small part of his living writing and lecturing about various forms of meditation. "TM is just one of the many."

Benson says that while he believes TM is completely sound, some 80 percent of the patients he treats for stress-related illness choose as their mantras words of prayer from their own belief systems—and get the same results.

Christians might choose a few words from the Lord's prayer. Jews might choose "shalom." Patients without traditional religious beliefs have had success with words like "love" or "peace."

But local TM center director John Boncheff maintains that "the state produced by TM is unique." Boncheff says that the aggregate of nearly 100 studies comparing TM meditation to other variations of the technique—findings that were published in a 1977 issue of the *Journal of Clinical Psychology*—supports his claim that TM is "approximately twice as great" in achieving maximum stress-reduction benefits.

Source: Ramsey Flynn, *The Washingtonian* (February 1990), pp. 130–132.

Systolic: The pumping phase of the heartbeat, reflected in the first or higher number of the blood pressure reading.

Diastolic: The filling phase of the heartbeat, reflected in the second or lower number of the blood pressure reading.

PROGRESSIVE RELAXATION

Progressive, or neuromuscular, relaxation is a technique designed to bring about a state of deep muscle relaxation. First described by a Chicago physician, Edmond Jacobson, in his book *Progressive Relaxation,* this technique has had excellent results in the treatment of insomnia, hypertension, tension headaches,

The Major Muscle Groups

1. Dominant Hand and Forearm
2. Dominant Biceps
3. Nondominant Hand and Forearm
4. Nondominant Biceps
5. Forehead
6. Upper Cheeks and Nose
7. Lower Cheeks and Jaws
8. Neck and Throat
9. Chest, Shoulders, and Upper Back
10. Abdominal or Stomach Region
11. Dominant Thigh
12. Dominant Calf
13. Dominant Foot
14. Nondominant Thigh
15. Nondominant Calf
16. Nondominant Foot

Note: Dominance corresponds to "handedness." Thus, if you are right-handed, your dominant side is your right side, and your left side is nondominant. If you are left-handed, your left side is dominant, and your right side is nondominant.

anxiety, and general autonomic nervous system arousal. In addition, it can help you develop a healthier, calmer attitude, which can make you less susceptible to a dramatic stress response. [3] Finally, progressive relaxation provides both a method for identifying tense muscles and a means to relax them.

The procedure involves getting into a comfortable position in a quiet environment and then systematically tensing and relaxing all the major muscle groups. (See "The Major Muscle Groups" above.) Through this process, you can learn to distinguish tense muscles from relaxed ones. In addition, you can acquire the skill to relax muscles that seem tense.

To experience progressive relaxation, clench your fist as tightly as possible. Then clench it tighter and tighter. Hold this tight fist for 10 seconds, noting the uncomfortable tense feeling. Now, relax your fist. Notice the blood flowing through it and the complete feeling of relaxation. Let it relax more and more. If you repeat this procedure for the various muscle groups in the arms, legs, trunk, shoulders, and head, you can reach a state of deep muscle relaxation.

The eventual goal of progressive relaxation is to be able to relax without going through the tensing first. Once this is accomplished, people can choose to relax no matter where they are or who they are with.

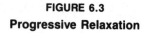

FIGURE 6.3
Progressive Relaxation

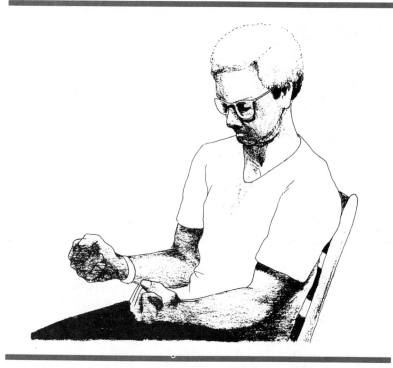

Progressive relaxation involves systematically tensing and relaxing all the muscle groups. To try this form of relaxation, clench your fist as tightly as possible for ten seconds. Then relax your fist. By repeating this procedure on all the muscle groups of the body, you can achieve complete muscle relaxation.

AUTOGENIC TRAINING

Autogenic training: A set of 6 exercises designed to reduce the alarm state that accompanies stress.

Based on the early self-hypnosis work of the brain physiologist Oskar Vogt, the German psychiatrist Johannes H. Schultz developed **autogenic training** in 1932. Using aspects of self-hypnosis, yoga, and progressive relaxation, the final states of autogenic training may produce breakthroughs of consciousness similar to those obtained through meditation. Autogenic training is an excellent alternative for those who, for whatever reason, are reluctant to engage in the Eastern meditative techniques. [4]

Autogenic Training: Standard Exercise Themes and Functions

Themes	Functions
1. My Arms and Legs Are Heavy	relaxes voluntary muscles of extremities
2. My Arms and Legs Are Warm	promotes blood flow to extremities
3. My Heartbeat Is Calm	normalizes cardiac activity
4. My Breathing Is Slow and Regular	regulates respiratory system
5. My Solar Plexus Is Warm	relaxes and warms abdominal region
6. My Forehead Is Cool	reduces flow of blood to head

Studies show autogenic training is effective in treating hyperventilation, bronchial asthma, constipation, diarrhea, gastritis, ulcers, spasms of the gastrointestinal tract, racing heart, irregular heartbeat, hypertension, cold extremities, headaches, **thyroid** problems, anxiety, irritability, fatigue, and sleeping disorders. It also modifies pain response and increases stress resistance.

The technique of autogenic training involves learning a set of standard exercises. These exercises are designed to reduce the alarm state that accompanies stress. There are 6 themes involved in the standard exercises. (See "Autogenic Training: Standard Exercise Themes and Functions" above.) The first theme, heaviness, is designed to bring about relaxation of the voluntary muscles of the body. First find a comfortable position in a quiet environment, then concentrate on the right arm while saying very slowly, "My right arm is heavy." After doing this 4 times, move on to the left arm and repeat the procedure. Finally, concentrate on both arms and say, "Both of my arms are heavy." Repeat this process for each part of your body. This exercise takes about a minute and a half and should be repeated 5 to 8 times a day for the first week. Gradually add new themes to the old ones until you have learned all 6 of them. For most people, this takes about 12 weeks.

Once you have mastered the standard exercises, you may choose to continue your autogenic training by learning a set of meditative exercises and/or special exercises designed to normalize specific problems such as cold feet or blushing. [5]

Thyroid: An endocrine gland located in the throat; important for regulating body metabolism.

BIOFEEDBACK

Western scientists once believed that control or manipulation of the autonomic nervous system function was impossible. They now believe differently. Modern biofeedback techniques have demonstrated conclusively that people can learn to control their autonomic bodily functions to some degree. [6]

Simply put, biofeedback is information about one's biological functions. Measuring pulse rate, blood pressure, temperature, and respiration rate are all biofeedback techniques. Biofeedback training uses highly sensitive instruments to measure minute bodily changes. The feedback from these instruments allows individuals to monitor bodily functions and learn to control or alter them voluntarily. The ultimate goal of biofeedback training is to teach people to change some bodily functions without using feedback equipment.

There are 3 main types of biofeedback training in use in the United States today: skin temperature, or thermal, biofeedback; muscle-tension biofeedback; and brain-wave biofeedback. Skin temperature is the most commonly used and simplest of the 3 types. You can detect changes in skin temperature as small as a tenth of a degree by using a simple finger hookup with a digital or meter display. The goal of skin temperature biofeedback is to increase blood flow to the skin voluntarily, thus increasing the skin's temperature. Skin temperature biofeedback has been used with considerable success in treating migraine headaches, Raynaud's syndrome (a disorder of the blood vessels, usually those in the hands and feet), and hypertension. In one study of 31 hypertensive people on medication, 87.5 percent demonstrated complete success at achieving normal blood pressure levels while reducing medication levels to zero. Unfortunately, these impressive results have not been duplicated in all studies. Other mental and physical applications include improving public speaking behavior, reducing menstrual cramps, and overcoming insomnia. [7]

The second major form of biofeedback training is **muscle-tension monitoring**. When a muscle functions normally, a series of electrical impulses travels to the muscle fiber. By recording this electrical activity, it is possible to determine the amount of tension in the particular muscle being monitored. The more electrical activity present in a muscle, the more tense the muscle; the lower the electrical activity, the more relaxed the muscle. These electrical impulses are very weak and are measured in microvolts (or millionths of a volt) as compared, for example, to

Muscle-tension monitoring: A type of biofeedback that involves recording the electrical impulses of muscle function in both normal and stressful situations.

(continued on p. 122)

I sank into the recliner and closed my eyes as the lights were dimmed and a blanket was wrapped around me. The therapist checked the sensors attached to my forehead and finger.

"Tense your forehead," she instructed. The soft, steady beeping of the electromyograph instrument increased in pitch and speed. "Now untense the muscles." The beeps faded.

Biofeedback: Beep If You're Tense

For an hour at the Neurology Center in Chevy Chase, Cathy Friedman's soothing voice worked down my body, from head to toe. She encouraged me to imagine growing limp and light, one muscle at a time. As my body unknotted, my mind drifted back to peaceful summers at my grandmother's place in Maine. The beeps disappeared.

I had done it. I had rid my body of tension. I thought about how well this experience would work in the story, about how the story was due the next week.

The beeps climbed back up the scale.

I had learned one basic principle behind biofeedback: Stressful thoughts increase muscle tension. Calm thoughts decrease it.

Using feedback is like taking your temperature. Biofeedback involves technology like the **electromyograph**, which measures muscle activity and lets you hear or see (on a video monitor) your body's signals. The idea is to monitor "involuntary" body functions, such as heartbeat, and bring them under some voluntary control. This allows you to ease a variety of tension-related ailments, including headaches, gastrointestinal disorders, and hypertension. Biofeedback is painless; it does nothing to you. The equipment simply indicates what is occurring in the body, much like a blood-pressure gauge.

If, for example, you suffer from tension headaches, biofeedback can help you recognize when your head, neck, and shoulder muscles are tense—even when you don't realize it—and help you practice relaxing them. Over time, you can learn to lower your pulse rate, cut short a migraine headache, even reduce the acid produced by the stomach. The sessions are sometimes combined with relaxation exercises and tapes.

Biofeedback therapists also help patients recognize the stressors in their lives, particularly negative "self-talk," says Friedman, director of biofeedback at the Neurology Center. Instead of stewing as you sit in traffic because you're going to be late, she explains, you could be saying to yourself, "I'll be only ten minutes late. I think I'll listen to some music."

Each of the ten to twenty weekly sessions costs $65 to $95, which is covered by many health-insurance policies. "People kind of get embarrassed that they're paying money and coming here to learn how to relax," says Friedman. "I say to them, if it were so easy, I wouldn't

A device called the Whole Brain Wave Synchro Energizer uses soothing sounds and timed light flashes to produce deep relaxation, the manufacturer alleges, by bringing the left and right sides of the brain into balance.

Electromyograph (EMG): An instrument used during muscle-tension monitoring to record the electrical impulses of muscular activity.

have a job. The trick to all of this is not trying too hard, because when you try to relax, you get tense."

Learning to relax, says Dr. Barry Gruber, director of biofeedback at the Medical Illness Counseling Center in Chevy Chase, requires practice and commitment. "We want that relaxation response to be so overlearned that it's like riding a bike," he says, "so that when they tell themselves to relax, whether they've just had a confrontation with their boss or are driving on the Beltway, they can maintain their physiological equilibrium."

In choosing a therapist, make sure that you are comfortable with the person, so you can relax. Most therapists prefer that patients be referred by their physician, or at least that they check first with a doctor. The therapist should keep in touch with your physician.

—*Sherri Dalphonse*

Source: *The Washingtonian*, February 1989, pp. 130–131.

Phobia: A persistent, intense fear of specific persons, objects, or situations accompanied by a wish to flee or avoid the fear-provoking stimulus.

Hyperactive: Denoting a behavioral pattern in children characterized by overactivity and inability to concentrate.

Electroencephalographic (EEG) training: A type of biofeedback that involves monitoring electrical impulses given off by the brain.

the 120 volts needed to light an ordinary electric light bulb. Highly sensitive electrodes are attached to an electromyograph (EMG), a biofeedback instrument that displays the electrical reading given off by the muscle. The subject uses this information to learn to reduce muscle tension. Often, relaxation or autogenic training exercises are used in conjunction with the biofeedback.

EMG biofeedback training has successfully treated tension headaches, anxiety, **phobias**, and insomnia. It has also helped people who chronically grind their teeth learn to relax their jaw muscles. Pregnant women have reduced their time in labor by learning to relax tense muscles. Stutterers, drug addicts, **hyperactive** children, and even dental patients have all benefited from EMG biofeedback. In addition, this form of biofeedback has shown promise in reeducating nerves and muscles damaged by injury, stroke, or disease. [8]

The third and final major form of biofeedback is **electroencephalographic (EEG) training**, which involves recording electrical impulses given off by the brain. This is accomplished by placing a set of electrodes at specific locations on the scalp. The electrodes are then attached to a recording device that provides a visual picture of the brain's activity. Because brain-wave impulses are very weak and can be easily misinterpreted, it is important to work with an experienced professional who knows precisely where and how to attach the electrodes and can filter out interference, such as that created by eye movement. [9]

FIGURE 6.4
Biofeedback

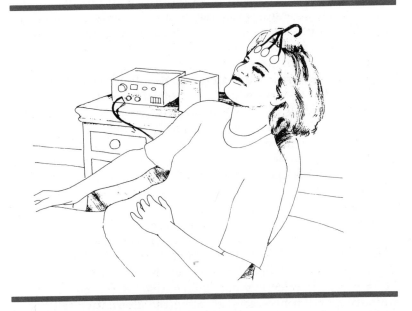

In biofeedback training, the subject is taught to monitor (through the use of highly sensitive instruments) the effects of the autonomic nervous system on bodily functions. The goal of biofeedback training is to teach the subject to alter some of these functions without using feedback equipment.

There are other types of biofeedback that have not been discussed here. Techniques involving heart rate, blood pressure, and **galvanic skin response** are all frequently used. Researchers are constantly looking for and often finding ways to monitor other bodily functions such as stomach-acid levels, blood chemistry, and even contraction of the **anal sphincter**. As techniques of monitoring become more sophisticated, biofeedback may provide solutions to many health/stress problems.

A PLAN OF ACTION: EFFECTIVE STRESS MANAGEMENT

In the final analysis, proper stress management entails following 4 general guidelines. First, managing stress is a highly individ-

Galvanic skin response: A type of biofeedback that involves monitoring the electrical impulses of the skin.

Anal sphincter: The band of muscle fibers that, when contracted, closes the anal opening.

ual process. What helps your best friend to control stress may be of little or no value to you.

Second, stress management must be multidimensional and comprehensive. A successful program involves strategies to control or modify stressors, alter individual perception, and modify the stress response. Selecting one strategy or technique alone probably will not work.

Third, stress management is a dynamic process. What works to control your stress today may not be effective in the future. When and if your stressors change, adjust your strategies.

Fourth, if they are to be effective, stress-management strategies must be followed. Strategies that are perceived as burdensome or as one more element to work into an already busy schedule will soon be abandoned. Make sure, therefore, that the strategies you incorporate into your life-style are ones you enjoy.

Making Decisions

Good decision-making skills are important in all areas of health, and stress management is no exception. Five steps are involved in good decision-making: (1) identifying the problem, (2) identifying all possible alternatives, (3) looking at the pros and cons of each alternative, (4) selecting one alternative to try out, and (5) evaluating and, if necessary, revising the alternative selected.

A variety of decisions confront those who are serious about managing stress. For example, how do you start to reduce or modify some frequent stressors? Should you begin by trying to change your Type A personality? Should you begin by altering your diet? Or should you begin by planning a more feasible schedule?

It is best to select the problem that you have the best chance of correcting successfully, and that will have the most positive impact in your life. Using good decision-making skills to set priorities for your life-style changes will help you to be successful.

You will also need to decide which stress-reducing techniques to use. There are many alternatives from which to select. These include biofeedback, transcendental meditation, progressive relaxation, and autogenic training. Find out as much about each alternative as possible, narrow them down, and make your choice.

Next, choose an exercise program. It is important to consider which activities you like and would probably stay with, as well as which activities will not involve (and possibly bruise) your ego. The cost of the activity, the time commitment, and the number of participants are other considerations. Along with reducing stress,

Sample Action Plan

I, _____, am going to initiate a comprehensive stress-management program by incorporating the following three strategies into my life:

1. To better control my stressors, I will: _____
_____
_____

2. To help alter my individual perceptions of stressors, I will: _____
_____
_____

3. To better manage a stress response, I will learn and practice the following skills at least three times per week: _____
_____
_____

I agree to do the above three strategies faithfully for one month. At that time I will reevaluate and revise my goals if necessary and continue realizing that stress management is a lifelong process.

Signed _____
Witness #1 _____
Witness #2 _____

Did You Know That . . .

A respected health manual says everyone needs 3 hugs a day, and studies have shown that hugging can relieve chronic pain, lead to a more positive outlook, and reduce stress in heart-attack patients.

some activities increase muscular strength, flexibility, or cardiovascular endurance. Activities that provide these additional benefits are highly desirable.

This text has provided some of the information necessary to make good choices about stress management, but interested persons should also research the programs available in their communities. Local health clinics, hospitals, YMCAs, local colleges, and recreation centers typically offer stress-management programs. Use the library to find more written information on the choices and talk to your friends, instructors, or colleagues. The more information you can obtain, the better your chances are of making a good decision.

Remember: You are a consumer of stress-management/stress-reduction programs and strategies. Act with caution. Many peo-

FIGURE 6.5
Managing Stress

Stress management techniques help people place stress and its causes in proper perspective. Choosing an exercise program is one important aspect of managing stress.

ple offering services are not qualified. Make sure you always ask for credentials and references. A background in psychology, counseling, or health promotion is strong evidence of quality, but no guarantee. Be wary of the single-strategy approach to stress control. There is no one technique that will manage your stress. A comprehensive, multidimensional approach is essential.

In the final analysis, the above decisions become important only after you have made the initial decision to take responsibility for your health and live a life-style conducive to wellness. Managing stress is vitally important to health, and only you can make the decision to control it before it controls you. 🔳

Glossary

A

Addictive drug: A substance that is physically habit-forming; stopping the use of an addictive drug results in withdrawal symptoms.

Adrenal glands: A small, triangular-shaped pair of glands located on top of the kidneys that secrete hormones, including adrenaline (epinephrine), directly into the bloodstream.

Adrenal medulla: The core of the adrenal gland; it produces adrenaline and noradrenaline.

Adrenaline: A hormone produced in the adrenal medulla that helps control the speed of the heart rate and the strength of the heartbeat, and alerts the body for action in times of stress. Also called epinephrine.

Adrenocorticotropic hormone (ACTH): A hormone, secreted by the pituitary gland, that acts on the adrenal cortex, stimulating growth and secretion of corticosteroids, including glucocorticoids. The production of ACTH is increased during times of stress. Also known as corticotropin.

Alarm reaction: The body's initial response to a stressor; the first stage of the General Adaptation Syndrome.

Alpha brain waves: Brain waves that occur at an average of 10 waves per second, characteristic of a relaxed state.

Anal sphincter: The band of muscle fibers that, when contracted, closes the anal opening.

Androgyny: The state of having a combination of both male and female qualities and characteristics.

Anxiety: An emotional state characterized by general uneasiness, apprehension, or fear.

Arrhythmias: Any variation from a normal heartbeat.

Assertiveness: The ability to declare and work on behalf of one's needs without alienating others or violating their equally valid needs.

Autogenic training: A set of 6 exercises designed to reduce the alarm state that accompanies stress.

Autonomic nervous system (ANS): The portion of the nervous system that carries messages from the central nervous system to the endocrine glands, the smooth muscles controlling the heart, and the involuntary muscles; includes both the sympathetic and parasympathetic nervous systems.

B

B-cells: Lymphocytes produced in the bone marrow that attack foreign agents dissolved in the blood or other bodily fluids.

B-complex vitamins: A group of 8 vitamins that primarily act as coenzymes, helping enzymes metabolize food.

Biofeedback: A method of learning to control involuntary bodily functions by mechanically monitoring one's own muscle tension, skin temperature, and brain waves, distinguishing between negative and positive responses, and trying to elicit more of the positive response.

Blood cholesterol: The level of cholesterol—a fatlike substance found in animal foods and also manufactured by the body—found in the blood.

Body language: Gestures, mannerisms, and posture that communicate a person's disposition.

C

Carcinogen: Any substance known to cause cancer.

Catecholamines: Hormones, including adrenaline and noradrenaline, that are released into the bloodstream by the adrenal glands as part of the stress response to stimulate the body and prepare it for action.

Central nervous system (CNS): The brain and the spinal cord.

Central serous chorioretinopathy: A form of blindness that can be caused by a stress response; it results when elevated blood pressure and the presence of certain hormones damage blood vessels near the retina of the eye.

Charlatans: Impostors or quacks.

Chronic disorders: Disorders that persist over a long period of time.

Circulatory system: The system consisting of the heart and blood vessels that maintains the flow of blood throughout the body.

Cognitive: The higher mental activities—perceiving, thinking, and knowing.

Comprehensive stress management: A stress-management approach that involves controlling the 3 elements that cause a stress response: the stressor, the perception of stress by the individual, and the physical and emotional reaction to stress.

Coronary heart disease: A reduction in blood supply to the heart caused by narrowing or blockage of the coronary arteries; often results in temporary or permanent damage to the heart muscle.

Corticotropin releasing factor (CRF): A chemical released by the hypothalamus that causes the pituitary to secrete adrenocorticotropic hormone (ACTH).

D

Depression: A mental state characterized by extreme sadness or dejection that persists for an extended period of time.

Deprivational stress: Stress caused by having too little stimulation or activity.

Diastolic: The filling phase of the heartbeat, reflected in the second or lower number of the blood pressure reading.

Distress: Stress caused by something negative or painful, such as a death in the family, being out of work, or failing a test.

E

Electroencephalographic (EEG) training: A type of biofeedback that involves monitoring electrical impulses given off by the brain.

Electromyograph (EMG): An instrument used during muscle-tension monitoring to record the electrical impulses of muscular activity.

Environmental engineering: Willfully taking command and modifying the stressors in one's own life.

Eustress: Stress caused by positive and enjoyable events, such as a job promotion, getting married, or competing in an important athletic event.

Exhaustion: The final stage of the General Adaptation Syndrome, characterized by the depletion of the body's stress-combating resources.

G

Galvanic skin response: A type of biofeedback that involves monitoring the electrical impulses of the skin.

General Adaptation Syndrome (GAS): The general pattern by which the body adapts to stress over time. As described by Hans Selye (1907–1982), the GAS has three basic stages: the alarm reaction, resistance, and exhaustion.

Glucocorticoids: The hormones cortisol and corticosterone, which are released from the adrenal glands and influence fat, carbohydrate, and protein metabolism. This includes increasing glucose production, thus helping to maintain the increased energy needs associated with a stress response.

H

Hardiness: A term used to describe a set of personality characteristics found in certain people who tend to cope well with stress. Hardiness comprises 3 distinct qualities sometimes referred to as the 3 C's: commitment, challenge, and control.

Hassles: Relatively minor but frequently encountered stressors, such as rush-hour traffic or long lines at the bank or store, that are sources of annoyance on an everyday basis.

Health spa: An often luxurious, residential, resortlike facility operated on a commercial basis that offers a variety of health-related services.

Hyperactive: Denoting a behavioral pattern in children characterized by overactivity and inability to concentrate.

Hyperglycemia: An abnormally high level of sugar in the blood that is associated with diabetes.

Hypertension: The medical term for abnormally high blood pressure.

Hypoglycemia: An abnormally low level of sugar in the blood that is often associated with diabetes.

I

Immunity: Protection against infectious diseases provided by the body's immune system and acquired through immunization, previous infection, or genetic predisposition.

Insulin: A protein produced by the pancreas that allows glucose to be taken up by a cell and used as fuel. A person without insulin or insensitive to insulin has diabetes.

Interleukin: A group of protein factors that act as a messenger between white blood cells involved in immune responses.

Ischemia: Inadequate blood supply to an organ, resulting in a disruption of normal function.

L

Lotus position: A meditating position in which one sits on the floor with knees bent, ankles crossed, and hands joined.

Lymphocytes: White blood cells that participate in the body's immune reaction to infections.

M

Mantra: A word or a sound that can be thought, imagined, or spoken during meditation.

Metabolize: To chemically alter substances in the body by breaking them down to produce energy or building them up to consume energy.

Muscle-tension monitoring: A type of biofeedback that involves recording the electrical impulses of muscle function in both normal and stressful situations.

N

Neurons: The impulse-conducting cells that are the functioning units of the nervous system; nerve cells.

Noradrenaline: A hormone produced in the adrenal medulla that causes blood vessels to contract when blood pressure gets too low. Often the release of noradrenaline is triggered by stress. Also called norepinephrine.

O

Overload: Stress caused by too much stimulation or activity.

P

Parasympathetic nervous system: The part of the nervous system that carries calming neural signals.

Perceived stressor: A situation or circumstance (stimulus) that an individual recognizes as stressful.

Performance anxiety: A stress-related syndrome, characterized by a fear of performing before an audience, that produces pronounced symptoms of anxiety; particularly severe cases may result in an inability to perform.

Peripheral nervous system (PNS): The portion of the nervous system other than the brain and spinal cord.

Phobia: A persistent, intense fear of specific persons, objects, or situations accompanied by a wish to flee or avoid the fear-provoking stimulus.

Pituitary: A small, pea-sized gland located at the base of the brain that regulates and controls the activity of the other endocrine glands (glands, such as the thyroid and adrenal, that secrete hormones directly into the bloodstream).

Premenstrual syndrome: A combination of emotional and physical symptoms, including irritability, tension, and fatigue, that occurs in some women prior to the onset of menstruation; popularly known as PMS.

Procrastination: The practice of putting off a required task or action in the absence of a valid reason.

Progressive relaxation: A technique designed to bring about total relaxation through tensing and then relaxing one body part at a time.

Pseudostressors: Substances such as the caffeine in coffee, tea, chocolate, and cola beverages that actually mimic sympathetic nervous system stimulation.

Psychological stressors: Stimuli that cause psychological (as opposed to physical) stress.

R

Resistance: Adjustments made by the body that allow it to maintain a high level of readiness in response to stress; the second stage of the General Adaptation Syndrome.

S

Self-actualization: A state in which one has realized his or her fullest potential by developing all of his or her capabilities to the greatest extent possible; associated with the personality theorist and psychotherapist Abraham Maslow (1908–1970).

Self-esteem: The value an individual places on him- or herself; one's feeling of self-worth.

Somatic nervous system: That portion of the peripheral nervous system that carries messages from the sense organs, and relays information that directs the voluntary movements of the skeletal muscles.

Stimulant: A chemical compound that elevates mood, induces euphoria, increases alertness, reduces fatigue, and, in high doses, produces irritability, anxiety, and a pattern of psychotic behavior. Stimulants include amphetamines, nicotine, caffeine, and cocaine.

Stress: Any disruption, change, or adjustment in a person's mental, emotional, or physical well-being caused by an external stimulus, either physical or psychological.

Stress response: The body's physiological response to stress that is triggered by the release of hormones; includes an increased heart rate and breathing rate, the diversion of blood to the muscles, and the release of fat from the body's stores.

Stressor: Any external demand or stimulus that triggers the stress response.

Stroke: Damage to part of the brain caused by interruption in its blood supply; stroke may result in physical or mental impairment or even death.

Sympathetic nervous system: The part of the nervous system that carries stimulating neural signals.

Systolic: The pumping phase of the heartbeat, reflected in the first or higher number of the blood pressure reading.

T

T-cells: Lymphocytes produced in the thymus gland that govern cellular immunity and assist the B-cells in producing antibodies.

Tachycardia: Abnormally fast heart rate.

Temporomandibular joint syndrome (TMJ): A disorder characterized by inflammation of the muscles, nerves, and tissues that surround the jaw joints.

Thyroid: An endocrine gland located in the throat; important for regulating body metabolism.

Time blocking: Setting aside specific periods of time for identified purposes.

Tranquilizers: Sedative drugs that have a calming effect, also known as minor tranquilizers.

Transcendental Meditation: A form of meditation that focuses on clearing one's mind by repeating a mantra.

Type A: A behavior pattern or personality type; the typical Type A individual is hard-driving, highly competitive, hostile, verbally aggressive, easily angered, extremely time-conscious, and unable to relax.

Type B: A pattern of behavior typical of individuals who are relatively relaxed or easygoing; often defined in contrast to Type A.

U

Uplifts: Positive events that create pleasure, serve as protection from stress, and counterbalance daily hassles.

W

Workaholic: Someone who compulsively devotes as much time as possible to his or her work and lacks interest in or is unable to find satisfaction in other activities.

Y

Yoga: A system of exercises originating with the Hindu religion that are designed to promote control of the body and mind.

Notes

CHAPTER 1

1. Hans Selye, *Stress Without Distress* (New York: J. B. Lippincott, 1974), 52.
2. Hans Selye, "History and Present Status of the Stress Concept," in *Stress and Coping: An Anthology,* Alan Monat, ed. (New York: Columbia University Press, 1985), 85.
3. M. Genest and S. Genest, *Psychology and Health* (Champaign, IL: Research Press, 1987), 92.
4. M. Friedman and R. H. Rosenman, *Type A Behavior and Your Heart* (New York: Alfred A. Knopf, 1974).
5. E. T. Smith et al., "The Test Americans Are Failing," *Business Week,* 18 April 1988.
6. P. L. Rice, *Stress and Health* (Monterey, CA: Brooks/Cole Publishing, 1987).

CHAPTER 2

1. G. S. Everly, Jr., and R. Rosenfeld, *The Nature and Treatment of the Stress Response* (New York: Plenum Press, 1981), 16.
2. M. Stein, "Stress, Depression, and the Immune System," *Journal of Clinical Psychiatry* (March 1989): 37.
3. Rice, pp. 50–52.
4. Rice, pp. 52–54.
5. Rice, p. 57.
6. D. A. Girdano and G. S. Everly, Jr., *Controlling Stress and Tension: A Holistic Approach* (Englewood Cliffs, NJ: Prentice Hall, 1986).
7. Rice, pp. 55–57.
8. D. G. Danskin and M. A. Crow, *Biofeedback: An Introduction and Guide* (Palo Alto, CA: Mayfield Publishing Company, 1981).
9. G. Hanauer, "Death by Stress?" *Omni,* August 1987, 22–23.
10. P. Siltaten, "Stress, Coronary Disease, and Coronary Death," *Annals of Clinical Research* 19 (1987): 96.
11. S. M. Levy, *Behavior and Cancer* (San Francisco, CA: Jossey-Bass Publishers, 1985).
12. Genest and Genest, pp. 127–128.
13. M. I. Finney, "To Your Health—TMJ: When Teeth Bite Back," *Nation's Business,* March 1989, 65.

14. D. Pine, "She's Got the Blinding Blues," *Health,* January 1988, 20.

CHAPTER 3

1. R. Forbes, *Life Stress* (New York: Doubleday, 1979), 16.
2. J. Alper, "Tranquilizers: A User's Guide," *Health,* November 1988, 86–87.
3. C. Lawson, "Stress Is the Name, and Management Is the Game," *New York Times,* 19 March 1988, A-34.
4. P. Wang et al., "A Cure for Stress?" *Newsweek,* 12 October 1987, 64–65.
5. C. A. Raymond, "Mental Stress: Occupational Injury of the 80s That Even Pilots Can't Rise Above," *Journal of the American Medical Association* (3 June 1988): 3097–3098.
6. Wang et al., p. 65.

CHAPTER 4

1. Girdano and Everly, p. 125.
2. D. Kipp, "Stress and Nutrition," *Contemporary Nutrition* 9 (1984): 1–2.
3. J. S. Greenberg, *Comprehensive Stress Management* (Dubuque, IA: William C. Brown, 1990): 78.
4. Girdano and Everly, p. 125.
5. Girdano and Everly, p. 127.
6. Kipp, p. 2.

CHAPTER 5

1. M. Davis, E. R. Eshelman, and M. McKay, *The Relaxation and Stress Reduction Workbook* (Richmond, CA: New Harbinger Publications, 1980).
2. D. C. Rimm and S. B. Litvak, "Self Verbalization and Emotional Arousal," *Journal of Abnormal Psychology* 74 (1969): 185.
3. J. E. Brody, "Increasingly, Laughter as Potential Therapy for Patients Is Being Taken Seriously," *New York Times,* 7 April 1988, B-8.
4. A. G. Sargent, "Androgyny as a Stress Management Strategy," in *Understanding and Managing Stress,* John D. Adams, ed. (San Diego, CA: University Associates, 1980), 89.

CHAPTER 6

1. "Exercise Restraint," *American Health,* September 1988, 40–42.
2. Davis, Eshelman, and McKay.
3. Everly and Rosenfeld, p. 116.
4. K. A. Pelletier, *Mind as Healer, Mind as Slayer* (San Francisco, CA: Robert Briggs Associates, 1977), 232.
5. Davis, Eshelman and McKay.
6. Pelletier, p. 54.
7. Danskin and Crow.
8. Danskin and Crow.
9. Danskin and Crow.

Resources

BOOKS

Braiker, Harriet B. *The Type E Woman: How to Overcome the Stress of Being Everything to Everybody*. New York: Dodd, Mead, 1986.

This book is for the high-achieving woman who is trying to excel in multiple roles and who thus becomes the victim of her own success. Braiker presents a stress-management program showing that women can be successful without killing themselves by trying to have it all. The author uses strategies, exercises, and mental workouts to help women juggle multiple roles and build better stress resistance.

Bramson, Robert M., and Susan Bramson. *The Stressless Home: A Step-by-step Guide to Turning Your Home into the Haven You Deserve*. New York: Doubleday, 1985.

Organization, communication, and tolerance are 3 important skills necessary to run an efficient home and produce a comfortable and tranquil home life. The authors show that sharing household responsibilities, delegating chores, setting goals and priorities, and working as a team are some of the ways for a family to establish domestic peace and make the home the one place in life where a person can always be relaxed.

Davis, Martha, E. R. Eshelman, and Matthew McKay. *Relaxation and Stress Reduction Workbook*. 3d ed. Oakland, CA: New Harbinger, 1988.

This book uses step-by-step instructions for progressive relaxation, self-hypnosis, meditation, imaging, biofeedback, deep breathing, avoiding irrational ideas, nutrition, time management, and more. It can be useful to anyone trying to adopt positive changes in behavior and life-style.

Green, Judith, and Robert Shellenberger. *The Dynamics of Health & Wellness: A Biopsychological Approach*. Fort Worth: Holt, Rinehart & Winston, 1991.

The authors provide a unique multidisciplinary approach to health and wellness with a strong focus on stress management. Many of the techniques mentioned by Randall Cottrell in the Dushkin book *Wellness: Stress Management* are covered as complete chapters in this book.

Hanson, Peter G., M.D. *The Joy of Stress*. New York: Andrews, McMeel & Parker, 1986.

The author uses an easy-to-read and often humorous style to provide insights into using stress to generate energy and achieve greater health and happiness. Hanson shows that stress, when mismanaged, can lead to alcohol and drug abuse, lost productivity, damaged self-worth, and illness. He provides examples of how to handle stress, how to make stress help achieve personal success, and how to increase the quality of life. Charts for vitamin and mineral supplements and examples of a balanced diet are also provided.

Howard, Elliot J., M.D., with Susan A. Roth. *Health Risks*. Tuscon, AZ: The Body Press, 1986.

The book provides a detailed discussion of the risk factors for cancer, heart disease, stroke, osteoporosis, diabetes, and stress-related problems, and the life-style changes that reduce the likelihood of developing them.

Jakubowski, Patricia, and Arthur J. Lange. *The Assertive Option: Your Rights and Responsibilities*. Champaign, IL: Research Press, 1978.

This is an older book, but the most recent printing is in 1990. The authors provide readers with the necessary skills to integrate more assertive behaviors into their lives. In essence, this is a "how to" book on assertiveness.

Mason, L. John. *Stress Passages: Surviving Life's Transitions Gracefully*. Berkeley, CA: Celestial Arts, 1988.

In this book the author discusses the different kinds of stress related to the different stages of a person's life. Mason discusses the kinds of stress that people face from adolescence to marriage to parenting to death. The author includes case studies and stress-reduction exercises.

Mattenson, Michael T., and John M. Ivancevich. *Controlling Work Stress*. San Francisco: Jossey-Bass Publishers, 1987.

This book provides a comprehensive examination of stress at the workplace and how to control it. The author covers the causes of work stress, how stress affects employees and the organization as a whole, how to improve organizational practices to minimize stress, how individuals can manage stress, and how to deal with legal issues related to stress.

Powell, Barbara. *Good Relationships Are Good Medicine.* Emmanaus, PA: Rodale Press, 1987.

This book addresses the importance of positive relationships. Powell discusses not only the value of good friends, partners, and spouses, but how to get along with others such as one's boss, coworkers, neighbors, and even the person behind the checkout counter. The author shows that being a good listener, understanding the feelings of others by sharing your own inner feelings, developing a sincere interest in others, and ignoring the minor failings of those around you leads to better relationships and less stress.

Rice, Phillip L. *Stress and Health.* Monterey, CA: Brooks/Cole Publishing Company, 1987.

This is an introductory book that provides a thorough and understandable discussion of stress and health. This book is of particular value to those who want more substance than is typically found in the popular literature but without the technical language of medical textbooks. The author presents detailed information to help the motivated reader develop useful stress-management skills.

Schafer, Walt. *Stress Management for Wellness.* Troy, MI: Holt, Rinehart & Winston, Division of Harcourt Brace Jovanovich, 1987.

The author begins with the assumption that stress is unavoidable. Schafer then presents research studies and practical advice on how not to respond to stressful situations and how to use stress in positive ways.

The Relaxed Body Book: A High-Energy Anti-Tension Program. The editors of *American Health Magazine,* Daniel Goleman, and Tara Bennett-Goleman. New York: Doubleday, 1986.

This guide is designed to help soothe tense bodies suffering from mental or physical stress, using gentle stretching and relaxation techniques. The book discusses how to control muscular tension for the entire body and how being physically relaxed aids mental relaxation.

Tubesing, Donald A. *Kicking Your Stress Habits: A Do-It-Yourself Guide for Coping with Stress.* Duluth, MN: Whole Person Press, 1981.

The book is designed for those who would like to change their life-styles and move toward less stress and more relaxation. Each chapter addresses a stress-related area and is filled with questions to help assess the kinds of changes a particular individual may need.

Witkin-Lanoil, Georgia. *The Female Stress Syndrome: How to Recognize and Live With It.* New York: Newmarket Press, 1984.

The author of this book maintains that because of their unique biology and conditioning, women are subject to physical and psychological stresses not suffered by men. They are at risk for all the usual symptoms of stress, as well as for a host of other stress-related ailments, ranging from premenstrual tension, headaches, and infertility, to life-threatening anorexia and crippling panic attacks. This book shows women how they can live with their stresses, offering reassurance and understanding while providing self-help exercises, relaxation techniques, and other therapeutic guidance to help women effectively manage their lives.

NEWSLETTERS

Harvard Health Letter is published monthly as a nonprofit service by the Department of Continuing Education, Harvard Medical School, in association with Harvard University Press. The letter has the goal of interpreting health information for general readers in a timely and accurate fashion. A one-year subscription is $21. Write to the Harvard Medical School Letter, 79 Garden Street, Cambridge, MA 02138, or call customer service at (617) 495-3975.

Healthline is published monthly by Healthline Publishing, Inc. The letter is intended to educate readers about ways to help themselves avoid illness and live longer, healthier lives. A one-year subscription is $19, or $34 for 2 years. Write to Healthline, C. V. Mosby Company, 11830 Westline Industrial Drive, St. Louis, MO 63146-3318, or call (800) 325-4177 (ext. 351).

Johns Hopkins Medical Letter, Health After 50 is published monthly by Medletter Associates, Inc., and covers a variety of topics related to healthful living. A one-year subscription is $20. Write to the Johns Hopkins Medical Letter, P.O. Box 420179, Palm Coast, FL 32142.

Lahey Clinic Health Letter is published monthly to bring readers timely, relevant information about important medical issues. Continuing topics include general healthfulness, natural and processed foods, depression, exercise, alcohol, prescription medicine therapy, major diseases, exercise, and more. A one-year subscription is $18.

Write to the Lahey Clinic Health Letter, Subscription Department, P.O. Box 541, Burlington, MA 01805.

Newsletter of the American Institute of Stress is published monthly and covers all topics of stress and the effects of stress on health. A one-year subscription costs $35. Write American Institute of Stress, 124 Park Avenue, Yonkers, NY 10703, or call (914) 963-1200.

University of California Berkeley Wellness Letter is published monthly and covers many topics, including nutrition, fitness, and stress management. A one-year subscription is $20. Write to the University of California, Berkeley Wellness Letter, P.O. Box 420148, Palm Coast, FL 32142.

PERIODICALS

American Health Magazine: Fitness of Body and Mind is published 10 times a year and covers every aspect of physical and mental well-being. In addition to feature articles, ongoing departments include Fitness Reports, Mind/Body News, Family Report, and more. A one-year subscription is $14.95 and may be obtained by writing to American Health: Fitness of Body and Mind, P.O. Box 3015, Harlan, IA 51537-3015.

Mind and Mental Health is published quarterly and offers a wide variety of articles covering all aspects of mental health. Written for the layperson, this British magazine has universal appeal and considers "mental health" to mean topics that deal with human relations, such as overcrowding in cities, abortion, and so on, as well as more traditional mental health topics. A one-year subscription costs $3. Write to the National Association of Mental Health, Maurice Craig House, 39 Queen Anne Street, London W1, England.

HOTLINES

National Health Information Clearing House, Department of Health and Human Services, (800) 336-4797; in Maryland, call (301) 656-4167. Operated by the Office of Disease Prevention and Health Promotion, this information and referral center's trained personnel will direct callers to the organization or governmental agency that can assist with health questions, whether they

are about high blood pressure, cancer, fitness, or any other topic. Available 9:00 A.M. to 5:00 P.M., eastern standard time, Monday through Friday.

Tel-Med is a free telephone service provided in many cities. Callers can ask for a specific tape number and have the health message played over the telephone. There are more than 300 medical topics to choose from, including topics related to maintaining a healthy life-style. Many states provide toll-free numbers for this service. Call the local information operator to find the nearest Tel-Med office, or write to Tel-Med, Box 970, Colton, CA 92324.

GOVERNMENT, CONSUMER, AND ADVOCACY GROUPS

American Cancer Society (ACS), 1599 Cliffs Road, Atlanta, GA 30329, (404) 320-3333
    The ACS supports education and research in cancer prevention, diagnosis, detection, and treatment, including the health effects of stress.
American Health Foundation (AHF), 320 East 43d Street, New York, NY 10017, (212) 953-1900
    The AHF is devoted to promoting preventive medicine. The Foundation conducts research into environmental carcinogens and nutrition, provides clinical research and service for adults and children, educates laypeople and medical personnel in the principles of preventive medicine, and investigates the medical costs of disease and compares them with the costs of preventive approaches. The AHF publishes *Health Letter* bimonthly.
American Heart Association (AHA), 7320 Greenville Avenue, Dallas, TX 75231, (214) 373-6300
    The AHA supports research, education, and community service programs with the goal of reducing premature death and disability from stroke and cardiovascular disease. The organization publishes several books, periodicals, and pamphlets related to maintaining a healthy heart.
American Institute of Stress (AIS), 124 Park Avenue, Yonkers, NY 10703, (914) 963-1200
    The purpose of the AIS is to further scientific investigation of the personal and social consequences of stress. The Institute compiles research on the relationships between emotional factors and cardiovascular disease, and be-

tween stress and the immune system, with specific emphasis on cancer. Research also focuses on stress reduction programs for industry, high-stress occupations such as police officers and executives, and pharmacological and holistic methods of stress reduction. AIS also seeks a definition of health that recognizes the need for harmony between the individual and the physical and social environments as well as the effects of positive emotions such as creativity, faith, and humor on health. The AIS disseminates information to individuals and publishes newsletters, books, papers, and speeches.

American Psychiatric Association (APA), 1400 K Street, NW, Washington, DC 20005, (202) 682-6000

The APA's membership includes psychiatrists who promote the availability of high-quality psychiatric care. The APA provides the public with information and pamphlets on stress disorders and other stress-related topics, assists state and local mental health agencies, and conducts educational programs for professionals and students in the psychiatric field. The APA library is open to the public by appointment.

American Psychological Association (APA), 1200 17th Street, NW, Washington, DC 20036, (202) 955-7660

The APA's membership includes professional psychologists and educators. The organization supports research, training, and professional services. The APA works toward improving the qualifications, training programs, and competence of psychologists and monitors federal legislation on mental health issues.

High Blood Pressure Information Center (HBPIC), 120/80 National Institutes of Health, Bethesda, MD 20205, (301) 652-7700

The HBPIC provides information on the detection, diagnosis, and management of high blood pressure to consumers and health professionals. The center identifies, collects, organizes, and disseminates information in many formats. Its sources are monographs, journals, newsletters, newspapers, reports, audiovisual tapes, brochures, posters, and contacts with other health agencies and clearinghouses. The center also provides reference and referral services, consultants, a speakers' register, packets, searches on the center's data base and resources of other libraries and clearinghouses, and referrals to other sources.

International Stress and Tension Control Association (ISTC), c/o Dr. F. J. McGuigan, Institute of Stress Management, U.S. International University, 10455 Pomerado Road, San Diego, CA 92131

The association disseminates scientific and technological information on tension control and seeks to incorporate systematic relaxation into everyday life. The ISTC publishes its *Newsletter* quarterly.

National Institutes of Mental Health (NIMH), Office of Communications and External Affairs, Room 12C-15, 5600 Fisher's Lane, Rockville, MD 20857, (301) 443-3783

NIMH conducts research and develops services to improve diagnosis, treatment, and prevention of mental illness. It also educates the public and health professionals about depression and its treatment, develops workplace educational programs, and produces and disseminates educational materials, including pamphlets and publications on stress and stress-related topics. NIMH is part of the Alcohol, Drug Abuse, and Mental Health Administration, a component of the U.S. Department of Health and Human Services.

National Mental Health Association, Inc., Information Center, 1021 Prince Street, Alexandria, VA 22314-2971, (703) 684-7722

This is a citizen's volunteer advocacy organization concerned with all aspects of mental health and mental illness. The group encourages research on mental illness and produces and distributes educational materials, including films that explain mental health issues. For a nominal fee (to cover printing costs), pamphlets about mental health and stress disorders caused by conflicts at work and home, illness, grief, and exhaustion may be ordered.

Index

Boldface page numbers refer to the pages in which the terms are defined.